# DISSECTION GUI

## III. THE RAT

WITH NOTES ON THE MOUSE

*by*

### H. G. Q. ROWETT, M.A.

LECTURER AT PLYMOUTH COLLEGE OF TECHNOLOGY

JOHN MURRAY, 50 ALBEMARLE STREET, W.

*First Edition* 1951
*Second Edition* 1952
*Reprinted* 1954, 1956, 1960,
1962, 1965, 1968, 1972

*BY H. G. Q. ROWETT, M.A.*

DISSECTION GUIDES

I. THE FROG
II. THE DOGFISH
III. THE RAT, WITH NOTES ON THE MOUSE
IV. THE RABBIT
V. INVERTEBRATES

HISTOLOGY AND EMBRYOLOGY

BASIC ANATOMY AND PHYSIOLOGY

THE RAT AS A SMALL MAMMAL

GUIDE TO DISSECTION

PRINTED IN GREAT BRITAIN
BY BUTLER AND TANNER LTD., FROME AND LONDON
AND PUBLISHED BY JOHN MURRAY (PUBLISHERS) LTD.

0 7195 1184 4

# INTRODUCTION

The rat is often dissected as an alternative to the rabbit. Though both may be taken as typical small mammals there are a number of important differences between them, notably in the proportions of the parts of the alimentary canal and the presence of seminal vesicles in the male rat. The details of the vascular system also differ enough to be confusing. The present volume therefore describes the rat alone and the rabbit is described separately. In some parts of the dissection the procedure for the two animals is identical, but in others it is totally different.

The diagrams show the dissection at successive stages. Owing to great variability in the amount of fat and in the position of some of the blood-vessels it is impossible to show the same degree of exactitude as in the drawings of the frog and dogfish. Wherever it occurs 'masking' fat should be removed with BLUNT forceps.

The dissection of the rat falls into three sections, (1) the contents of the abdomen, (2) the contents of the thorax and the neck, (3) the brain. For the first two of these sections the rat should be attached ventral side uppermost to a wooden dissecting board. Large wooden- or brass-handled pins are used for this purpose, but a supply of ordinary pins will be found useful for holding the various structures in place during the display.

With the exception of the brain, dissection is best performed on a freshly-killed specimen. Especially is this so for display of the alimentary canal and the diaphragm.

Before the brain is dissected the nervous tissue MUST be hardened with preservative. To hasten the penetration of the brain by the formalin a small section of the roof of the skull may be removed, see Figs. 41-44.

N.B.—When dissecting a freshly-killed rat there is always much capillary bleeding. The blood should be kept mopped up with a cloth so that the structures retain their own shade of colour and do not become uniformly reddened and thus more difficult to identify.

Diagrams of the parts of the skeleton of the rat are given as an appendix because they are not described in any of the common textbooks.

The rats used for dissection vary in size. A standard scale has therefore been chosen and all other scales are multiples of the standard. The standard scale as seen in Fig. 1 is about two-thirds the size of an average rat.

I wish to acknowledge my indebtedness to Mr. Nigel Bateman of the Animal Breeding and Genetics Research Organisation for checking the section on the skeleton. There is no reliable reference on this subject and I am very grateful to him for his careful inspection of the text and diagrams and for his suggestions.

# THE MOUSE

The anatomy of the mouse is so similar to that of the rat that separate instructions are unnecessary. The following points should however be noted :—

1. Because of the small size the tissues are more delicate and capillary bleeding occurs very easily. The mouse should therefore be dissected under water to wash away the blood and also to minimize the adhesion of parts.

2. Ordinary small pins should be used instead of dissecting pins to pin the mouse to the dish and may also be used to hold organs in place when they tend to float about. Be careful to place the pins *against*, not through the organs.

3. Anatomical differences of importance are :—

    (a) much larger preputial glands of a conspicuous yellow colour,
    (b) relatively longer intestines,
    (c) absence of ridges from the external wall of the colon (see insets to Figs. 7-9),
    (a) separate bile and pancreatic ducts (see inset to Fig. 9),
    (e) some of the lymph nodes differently placed (note especially the absence of the node mentioned in Fig. 11),
    (f) scrotal sacs very shallow so that the testes slip out of them easily,
    (g) renal and dorso-lumbar blood-vessels relatively further apart and right dorso-lumbar vessels posterior to the left ones,
    (h) much more masking fat in older mice than rats, making dissection of the delicate blood-vessels of the pelvic region almost impossible in some cases,
    (i) thymus gland more diffuse and more difficult to remove,
    (j) middle cervical sympathetic ganglion more anteriorly placed than in the rat,

4. While with care it is possible to see almost all the structures seen in the dissection of the rat, the smaller size makes this very difficult in the case of the pelvic blood-vessels and the roots of the cranial nerves. A lens should be used where necessary and the *extreme delicacy of the tissues should be remembered throughout.*

# CONTENTS

# GENERAL DIRECTIONS IN PREPARATION FOR DISSECTION OF THE ABDOMEN, THORAX OR NECK

If desired, the skin may be removed completely, but it is more usual to lay it back as shown in Figs. 1–3.

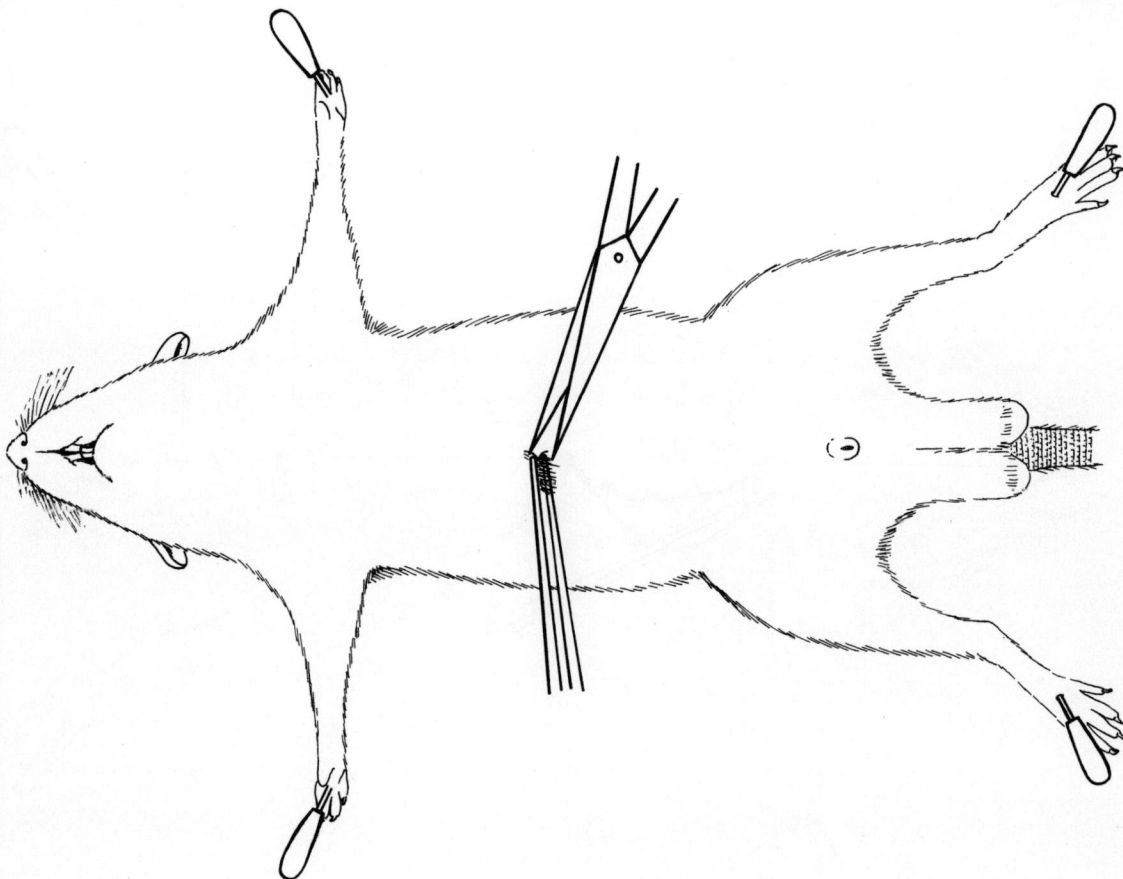

Fig. 1

Lay the rat ventral side uppermost on a dissecting board and attach it in spread-eagle position by means of strong dissecting pins through the fore- and hind-feet. Place each pin at an angle to the strain put on it. Lift the skin in the mid-ventral line and cut as indicated.

*GENERAL DIRECTIONS IN PREPARATION*

### Fig. 2a. Male

Slit the skin along the mid-ventral line.
N.B. Keep the scissors as horizontal as possible to avoid cutting the body-wall under the skin.
Continue the cut forwards to the level of the lower lip and backwards around the penis and between the scrotal sacs.

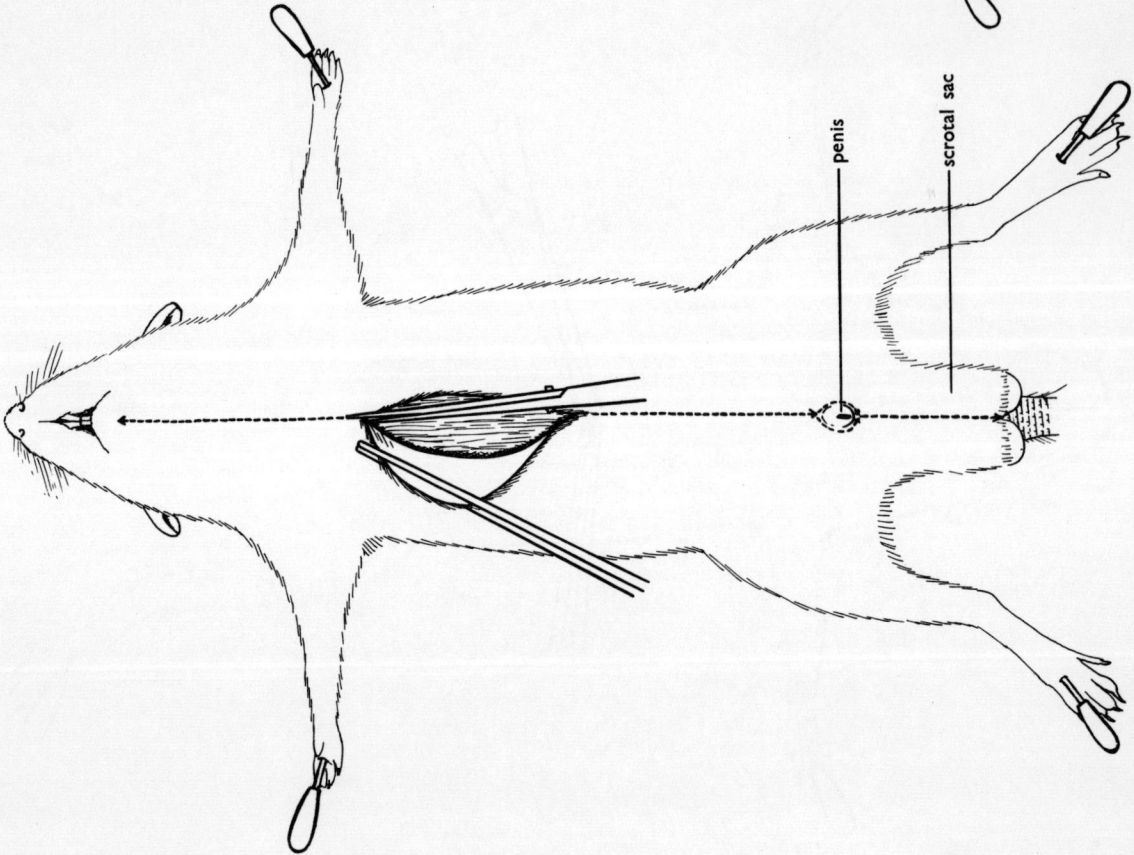

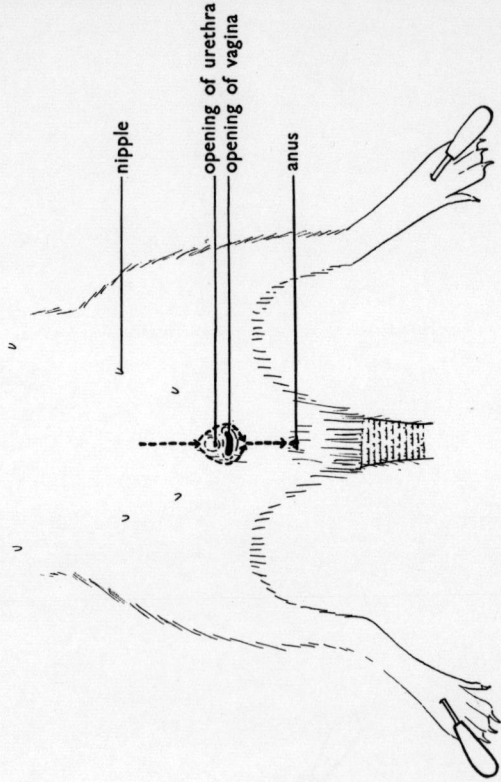

nipple

opening of urethra
opening of vagina

anus

### Fig. 2b. Female

Cut the skin as described for the male, but continue the cut backwards as far as the anus, passing on either side of the urinary and genital apertures.

penis

scrotal sac

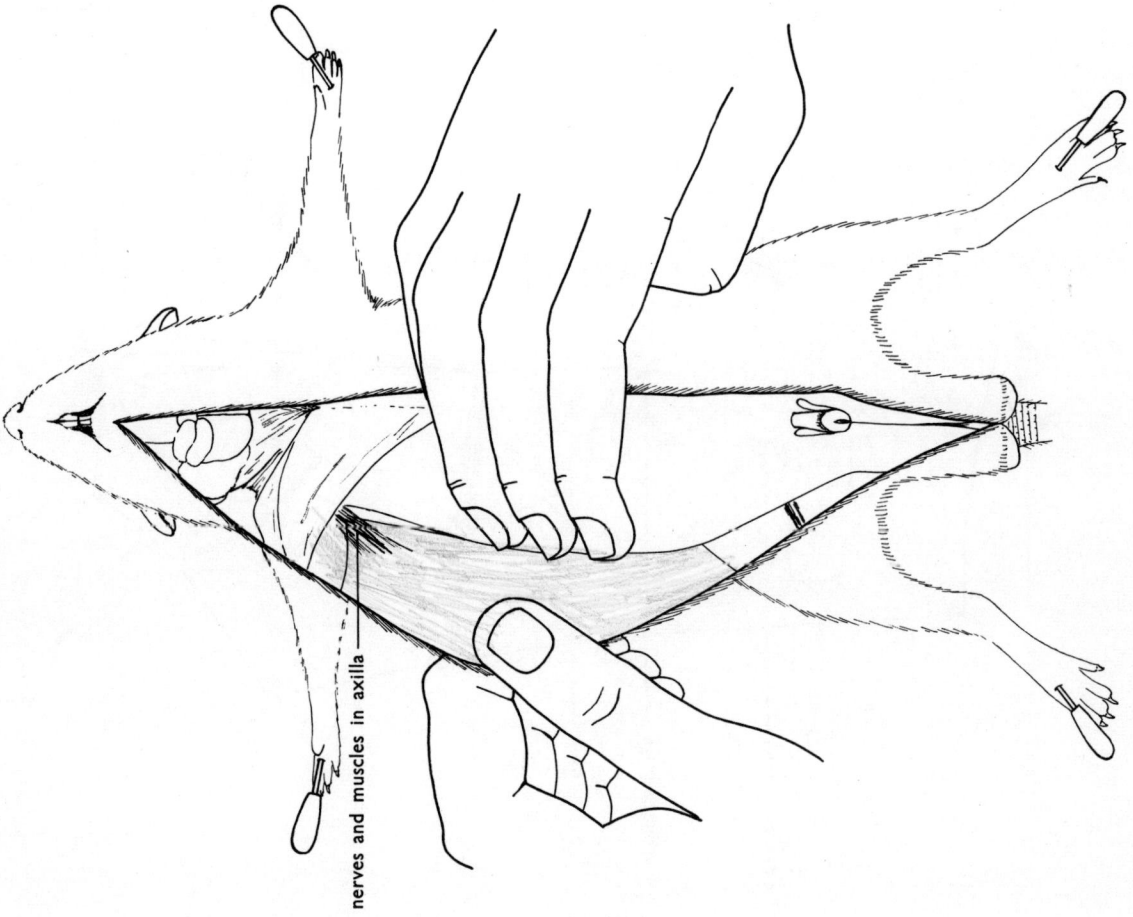

**Fig. 3**

Pull aside the skin, loosening it from the body-wall by using the fingers as shown.

N.B. Be careful not to tear the nerves and muscles in the axillary region.

nerves and muscles in axilla

## SECTION I—THE ABDOMEN

### (a) OPENING UP THE ABDOMINAL CAVITY

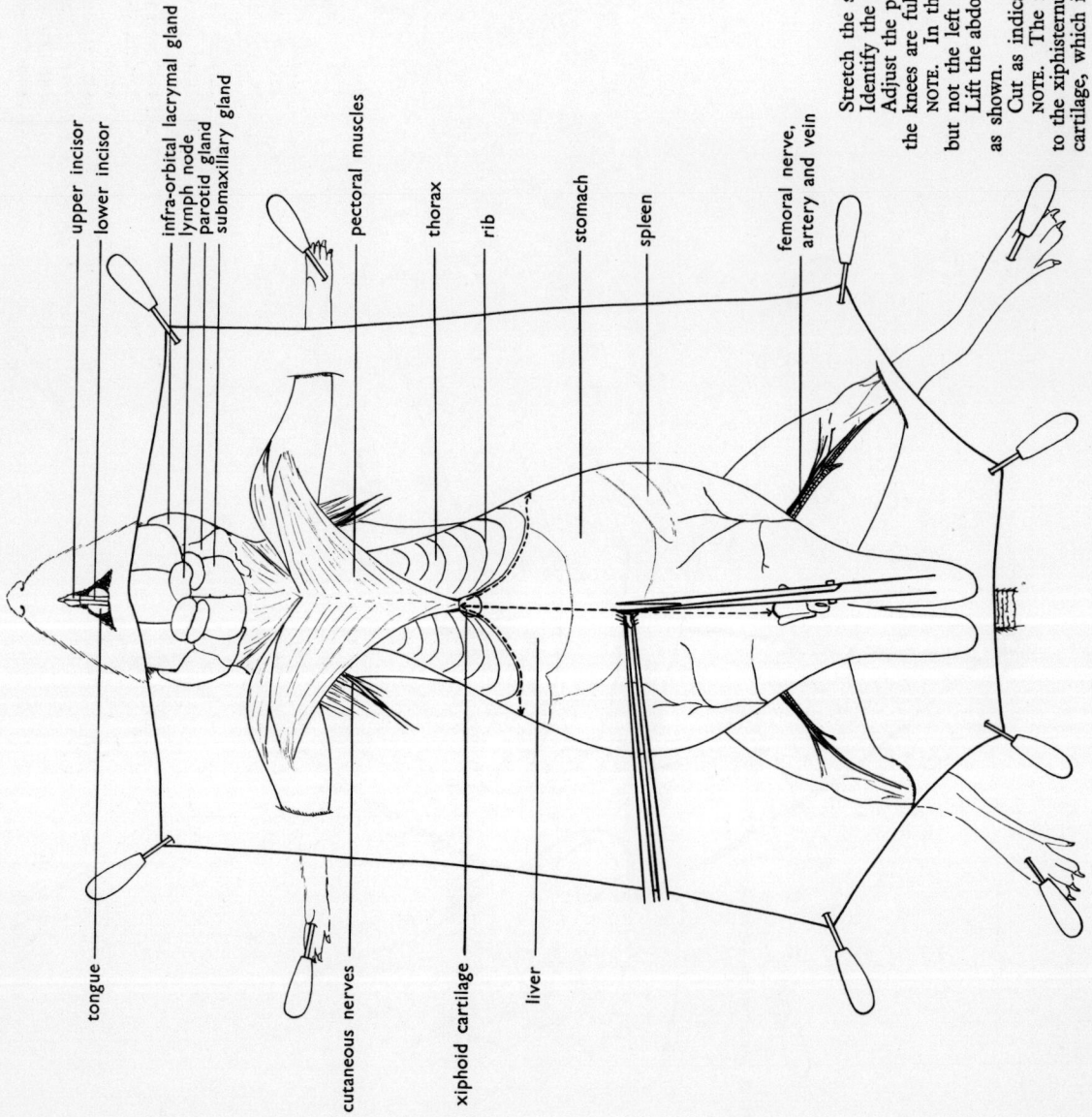

Fig. 4a.  Male

Stretch the skin and pin it back as shown.
Identify the parts labelled.
Adjust the positions of the pins through the legs so that
the knees are fully extended.
NOTE.  In the diagram this has been done on the right
but not the left side to show the difference.
Lift the abdominal wall with forceps and make an incision
as shown.
Cut as indicated by the dotted lines.
NOTE.  The muscles of the abdominal wall are attached
to the xiphisternum.  They can be lifted clear of the xiphoid
cartilage, which is therefore not cut.

upper incisor
lower incisor
infra-orbital lacrymal gland
lymph node
parotid gland
submaxillary gland
pectoral muscles
thorax
rib
stomach
spleen
femoral nerve,
artery and vein

tongue
cutaneous nerves
xiphoid cartilage
liver

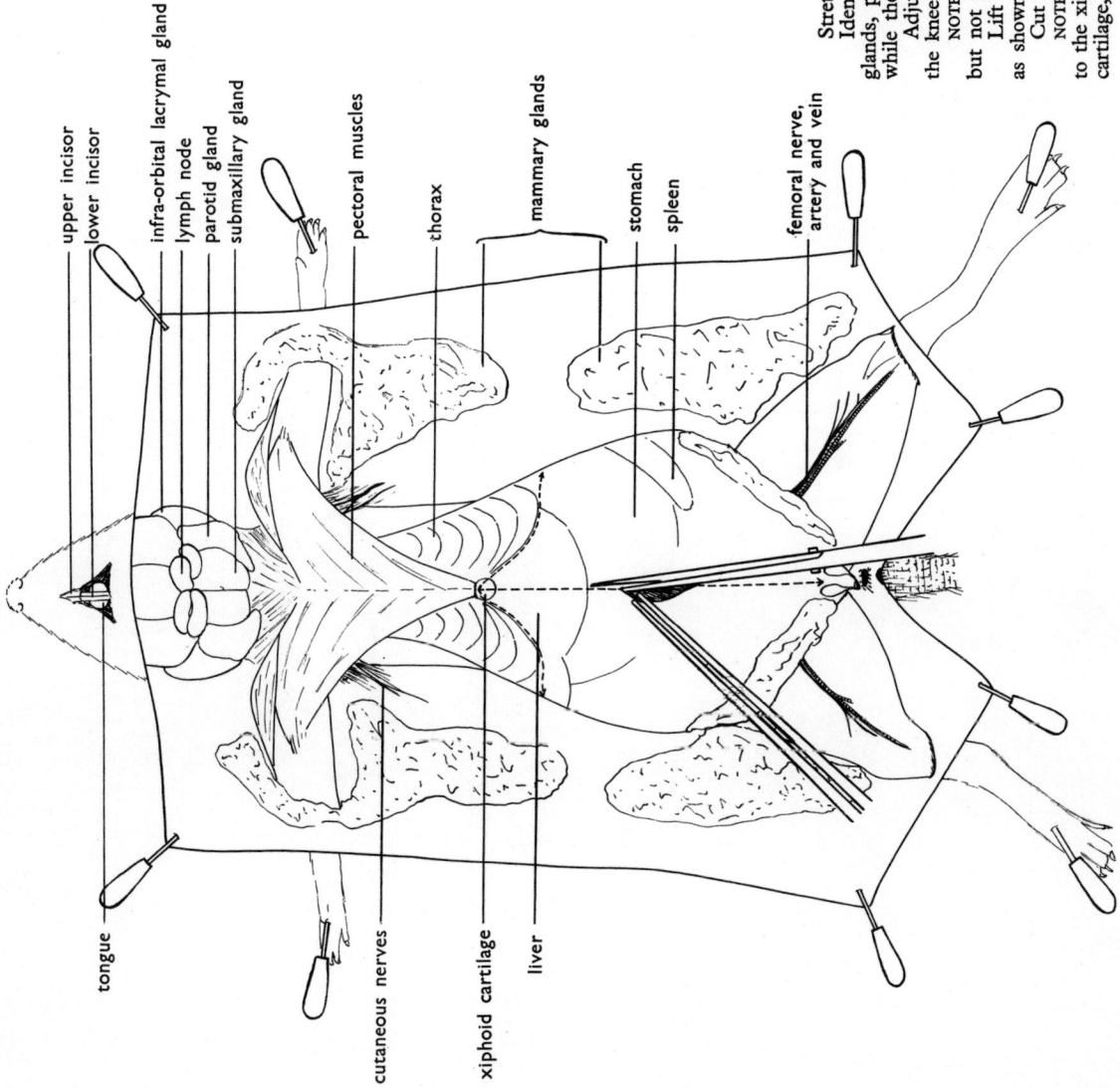

upper incisor
lower incisor

infra-orbital lacrymal gland
lymph node
parotid gland
submaxillary gland

pectoral muscles

thorax

mammary glands

stomach
spleen

femoral nerve, artery and vein

tongue

cutaneous nerves

xiphoid cartilage

liver

**Fig. 4b. Female**

Stretch the skin and pin it out as shown.
Identify the parts labelled, noticing especially the mammary glands, parts of which usually remain in the inguinal region while the rest comes away with the skin.

Adjust the positions of the pins through the legs so that the knees are fully extended.

NOTE. In the diagram this has been done on the right but not the left side to show the difference.

Lift the abdominal wall with forceps and make an incision as shown.

Cut as indicated by the dotted lines.

NOTE. The muscles of the abdominal wall are attached to the xiphisternum. They can be lifted clear of the xiphoid cartilage, which is therefore not cut.

## THE ABDOMEN

### (b) THE ALIMENTARY CANAL

A male rat is shown throughout this section with the exception of Fig. 5b, but the procedure is identical in the female.

With care, the abdominal parts of the alimentary canal can be displayed without further use of instruments. All that is necessary is the rearrangement of the parts so that they can be seen clearly.

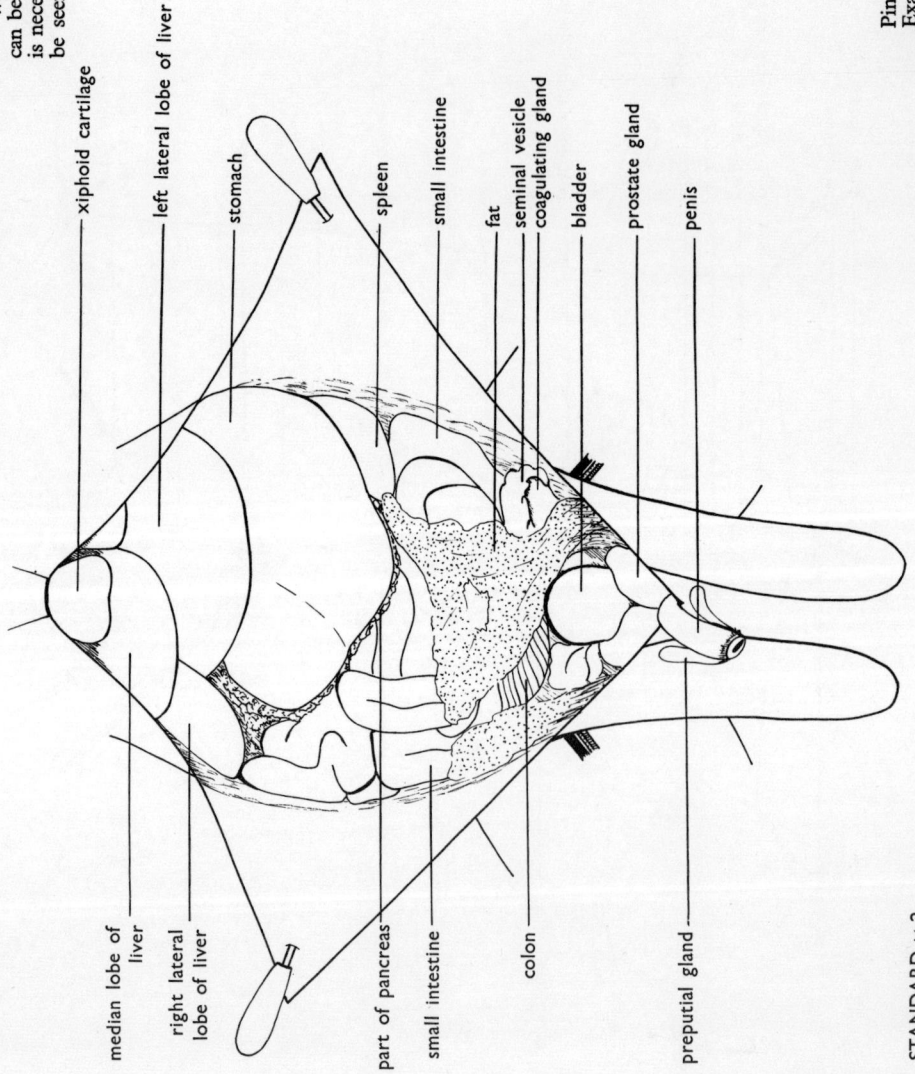

**Fig. 5a. Male**

Pin aside the abdominal wall.
Examine the contents of the abdominal cavity in the undisturbed condition.

STANDARD × 2

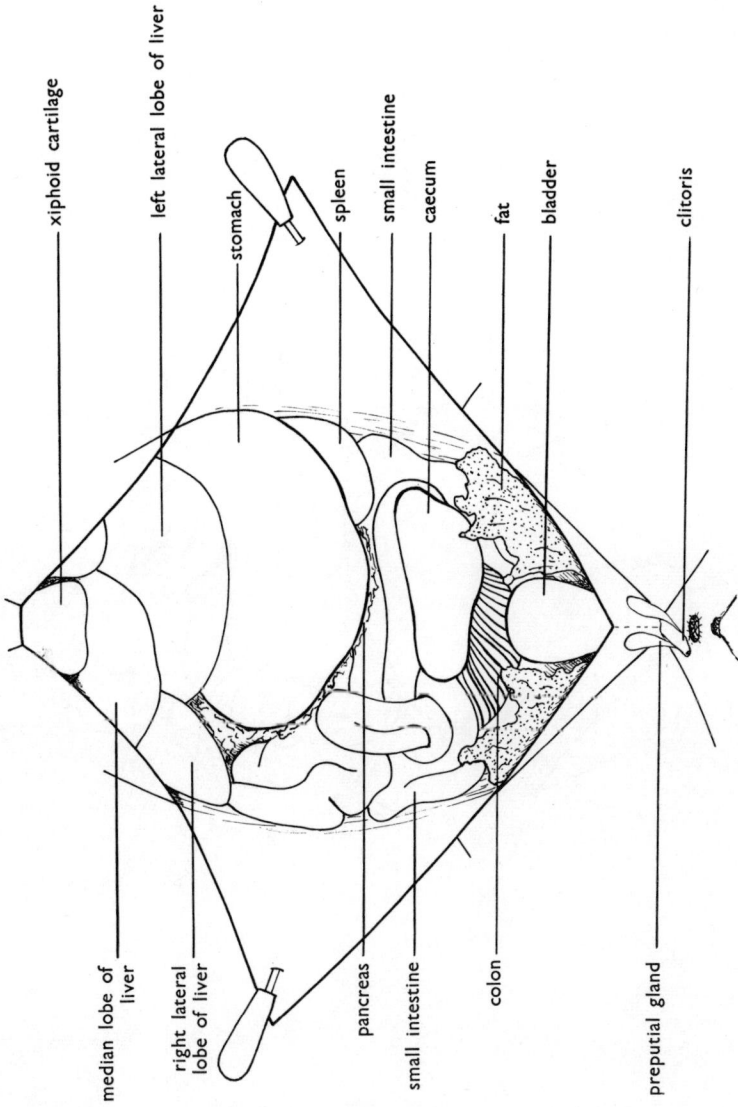

**Fig. 5b. Female**

Pin aside the abdominal wall.
Examine the contents of the abdominal cavity in the
undisturbed condition.

STANDARD × 2

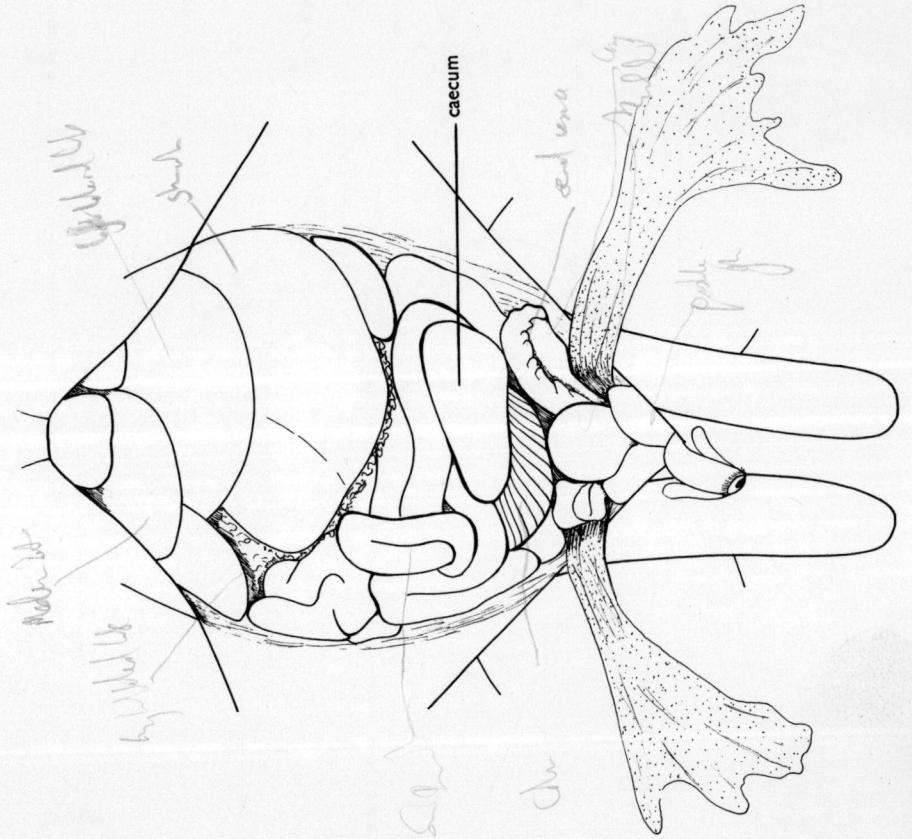

**Fig. 6**
Lay aside the fat bodies.

caecum

STANDARD × 2

small intestine
colon
caecum

duodenum

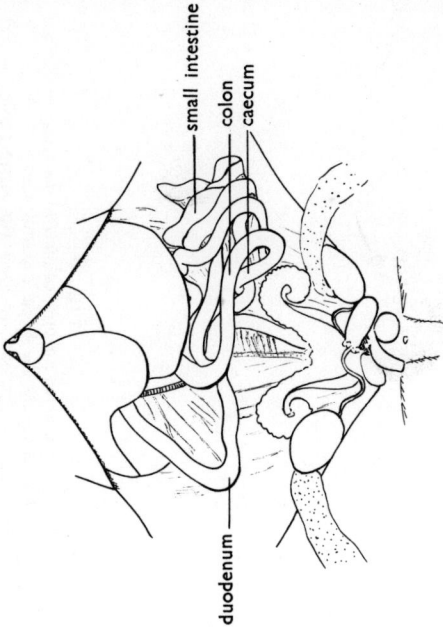

INSET—THE MOUSE

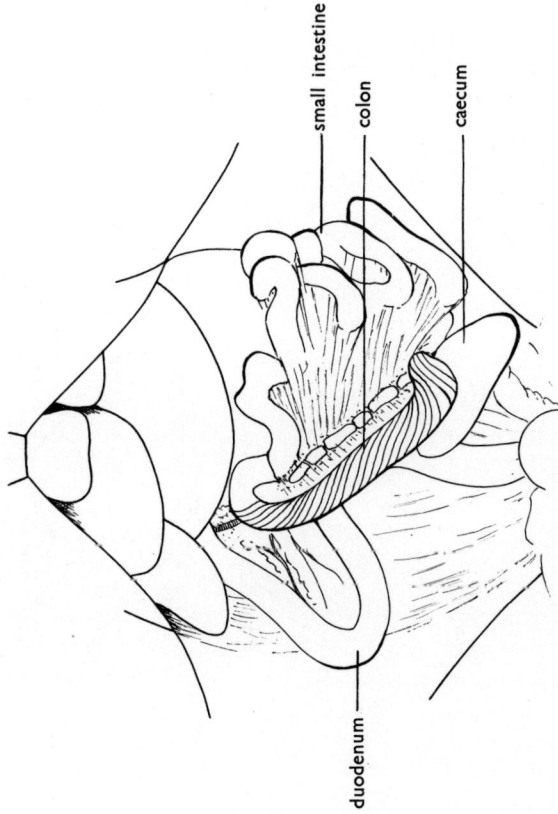

STANDARD × 2

small intestine
colon

caecum

duodenum

**Fig. 7**

Move the bulk of the intestines to YOUR right. Find the
duodenum and colon.
NOTE. There is some adhesion of their mesenteries.

*THE ABDOMEN*

hepatic portal vein

small intestine crossing
large intestine

turn over

hepatic portal vein

small intestine crossing
large intestine
lymph node

turn over

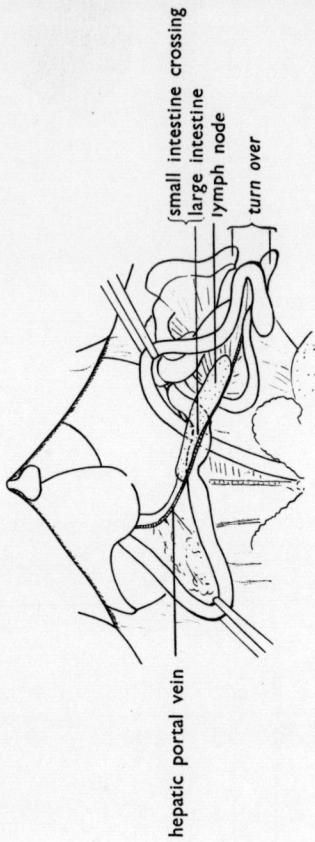

*INSET—THE MOUSE*

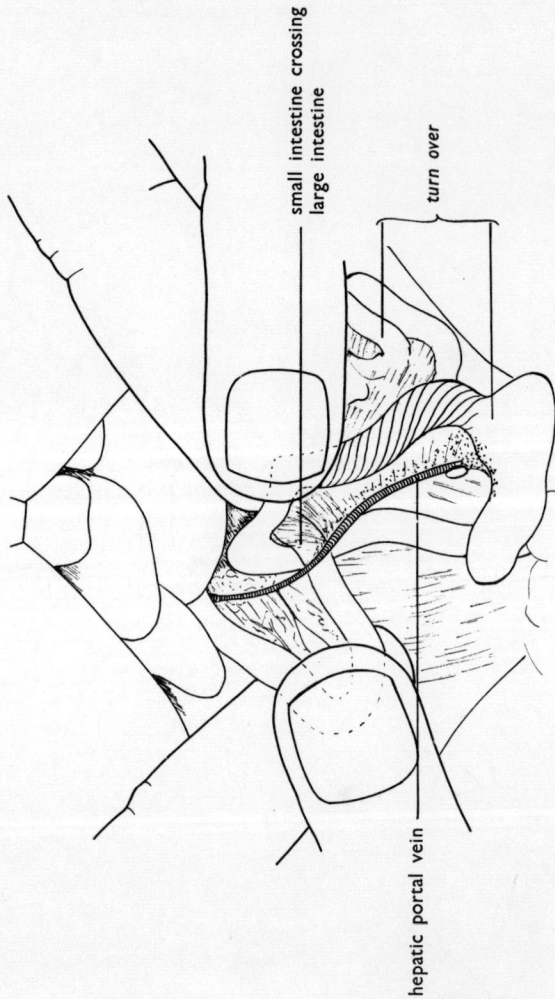

STANDARD × 2

**Fig. 8**

Grip the duodenum and colon and carefully pull them apart, thus exposing the hepatic portal vein.

N.B. BE CAREFUL NOT TO TEAR THE MESENTERIES.

Notice the way in which the small and large intestines are twisted over one another.

Turn the bulk of the intestines over to undo this twist.

14

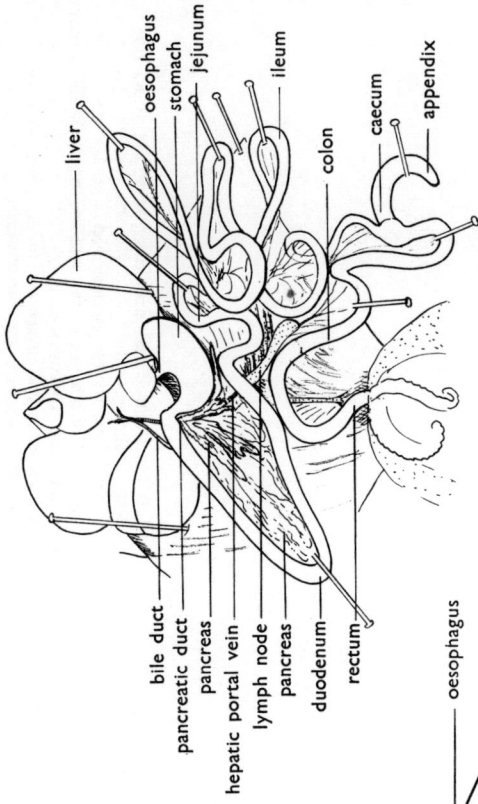

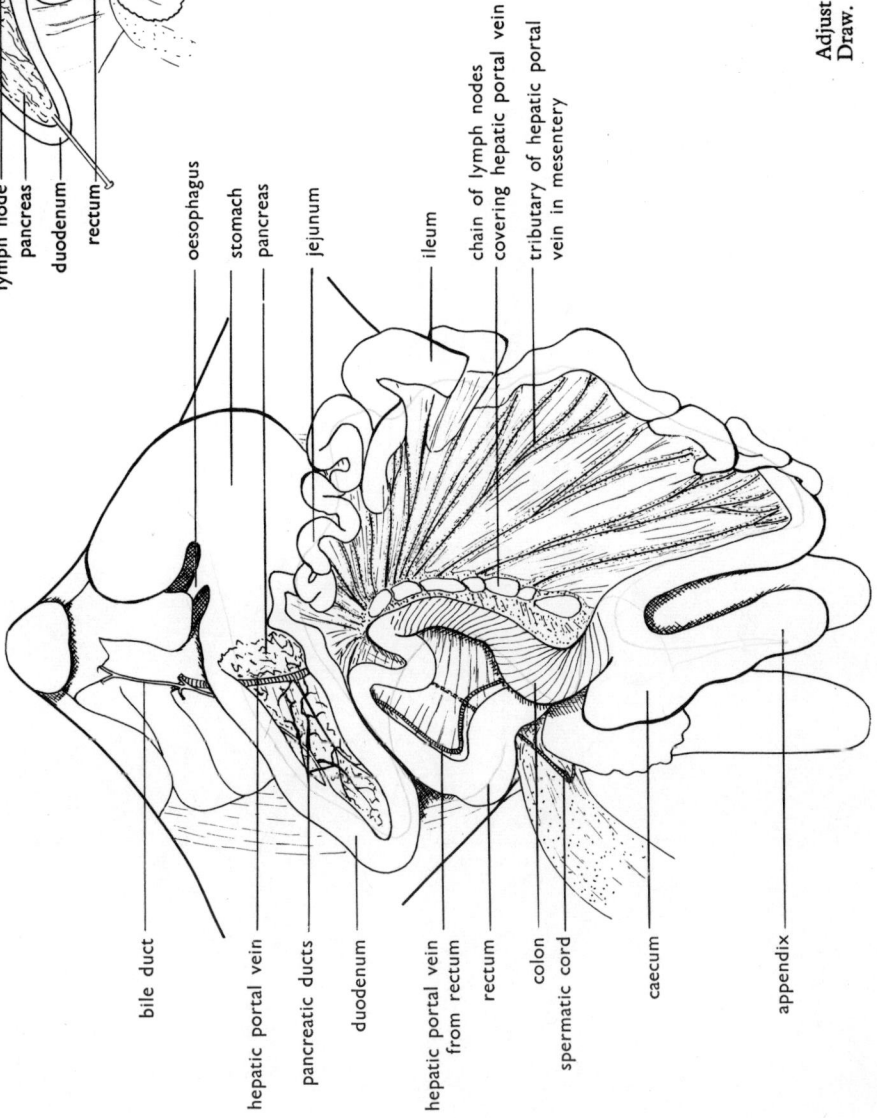

INSET—THE MOUSE

STANDARD × 2

**Fig. 9**

Adjust the positions of the structures as shown.
Draw.

liver
oesophagus
stomach
jejunum
ileum
colon
caecum
appendix

bile duct
pancreatic duct
pancreas
hepatic portal vein
lymph node
pancreas
duodenum
rectum

oesophagus
stomach
pancreas
jejunum
ileum
chain of lymph nodes
covering hepatic portal vein
tributary of hepatic portal
vein in mesentery

bile duct
hepatic portal vein
pancreatic ducts
duodenum
hepatic portal vein
from rectum
rectum
colon
spermatic cord
caecum
appendix

15

## THE ABDOMEN

(c) THE SOLAR PLEXUS

The dissection of the solar plexus is often omitted by elementary students, but is not difficult if sufficient care be taken. It is very important to AVOID CAPILLARY BLEEDING as far as possible and to mop up any that may occur.

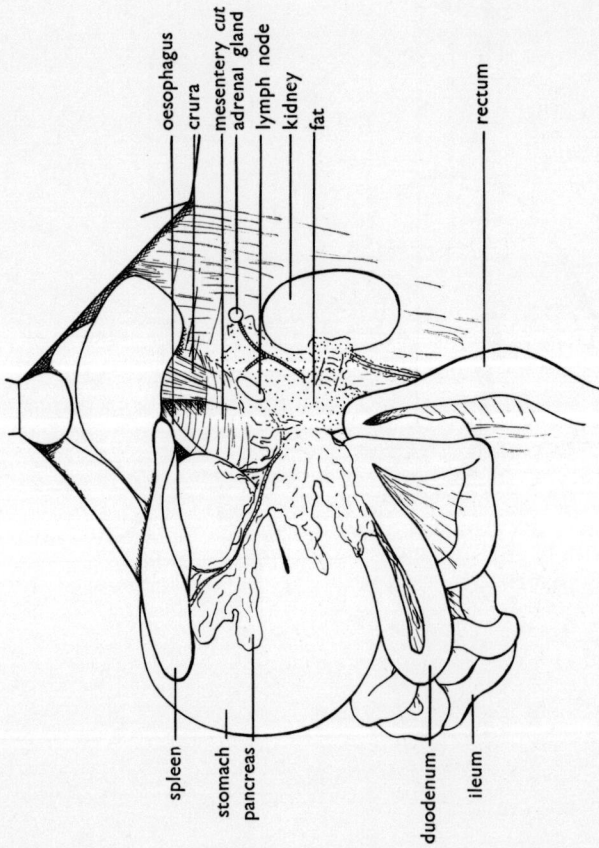

Labels on figure:
spleen, stomach, pancreas, duodenum, ileum, oesophagus, crura, mesentery cut, adrenal gland, lymph node, kidney, fat, rectum

### Fig. 10

Lay the stomach and intestines over to the RIGHT SIDE OF THE RAT as shown.

Identify the structures indicated.

NOTE. The amount of fat, and consequently the amount of masking, is very variable.

Cut or tear the mesentery holding the stomach, being careful not to damage any blood-vessels.

STANDARD × 2

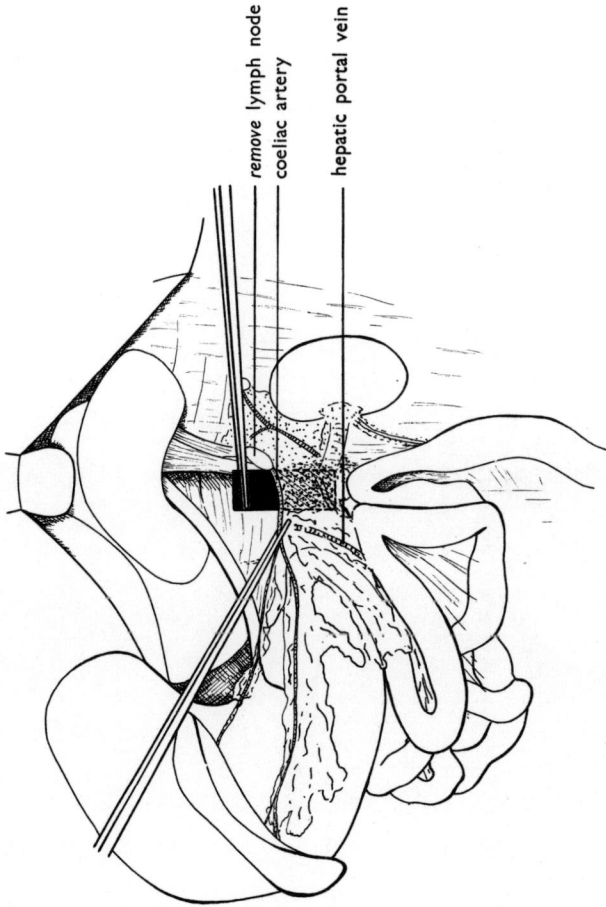

remove lymph node
coeliac artery
hepatic portal vein

**Fig. 11**

Adjust the position of the stomach as shown.
Identify and lift up the coeliac artery.
Insert a small piece of black paper behind the artery and
the region immediately posterior to it.
Remove the lymph node with forceps.
With blunt forceps gently pluck away the fat from the
area overlying the black paper.
N.B. Watch for the structures shown in Fig. 12.

STANDARD × 2

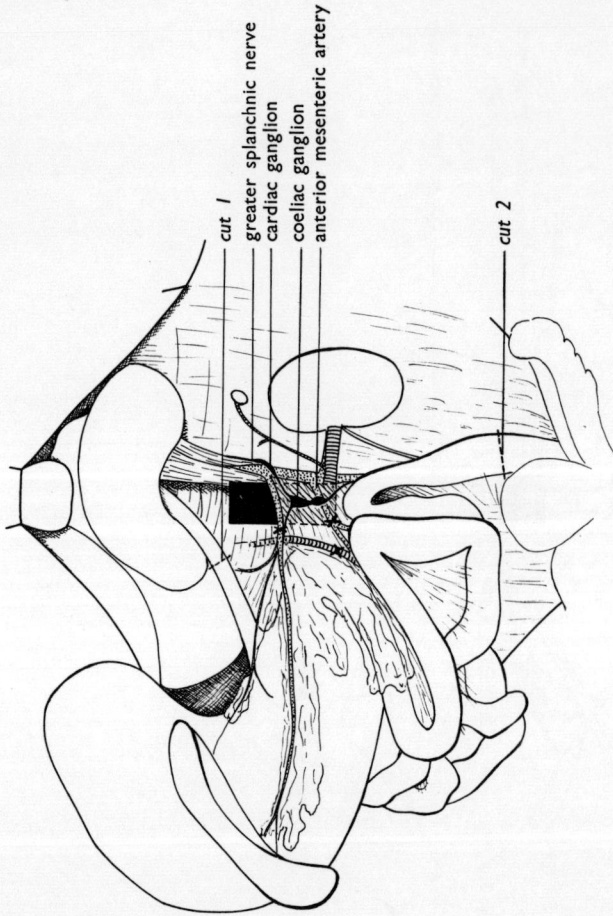

cut 1
greater splanchnic nerve
cardiac ganglion
coeliac ganglion
anterior mesenteric artery

cut 2

STANDARD × 2

## Fig. 12

Observe and draw the solar plexus.

(d) REMOVAL OF THE ALIMENTARY CANAL

The alimentary canal must be removed before any dissection of the urinogenital system and abdominal blood-vessels.

Ligature the coeliac and anterior mesenteric arteries and the hepatic portal vein in the positions indicated by X. Cut each vessel distal to the ligature.

Cut the oesophagus—cut 1.

Cut the rectum—cut 2.

NOTE. The posterior mesenteric artery will be destroyed if the rectum is cut too near the pelvis.

Gently tear the mesentery to remove the alimentary canal.

## THE ABDOMEN

(e) THE MALE URINOGENITAL SYSTEM

Before dissecting this system the alimentary canal must be removed as shown in Fig. 12.

There is considerable variation in the amount and fat and also in the finer details of the distribution of blood-vessels which, though they are shown in the following diagrams, need not be cleared till later.

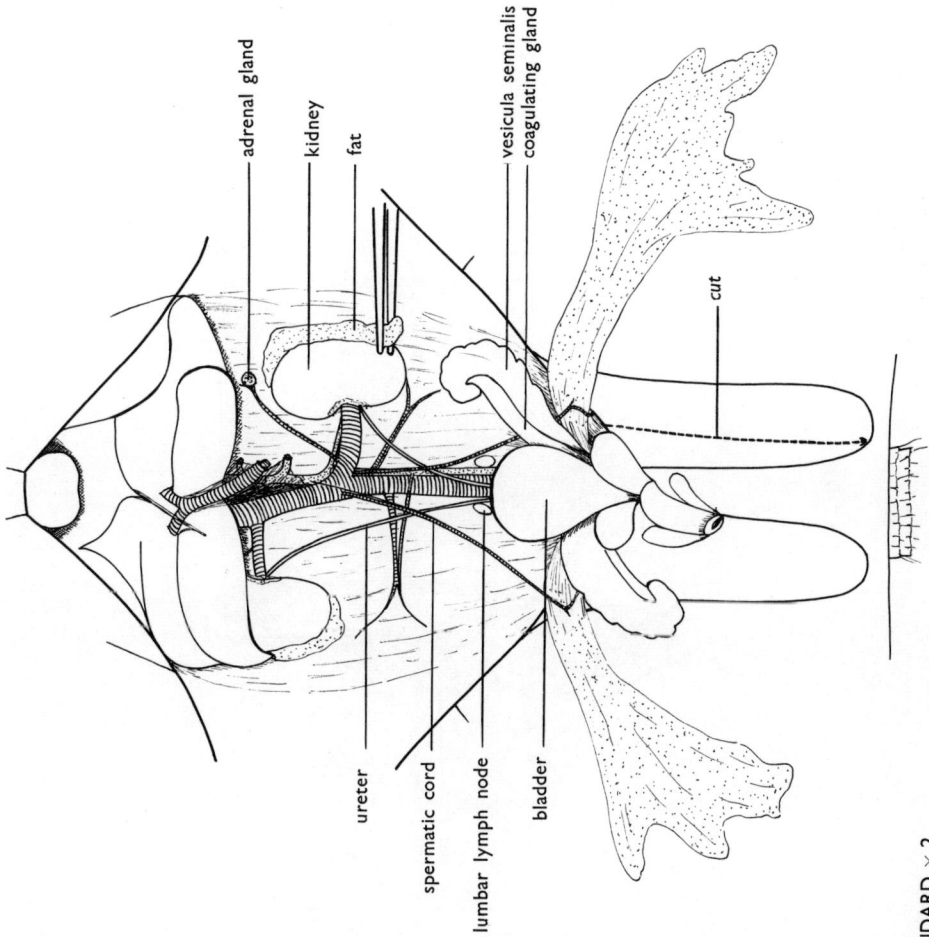

**Fig. 13**

Remove the fat from the kidneys, using blunt forceps as shown.

Similarly clear the ureters.

Cut through the ventral wall of the scrotal sac along the line indicated.

STANDARD × 2

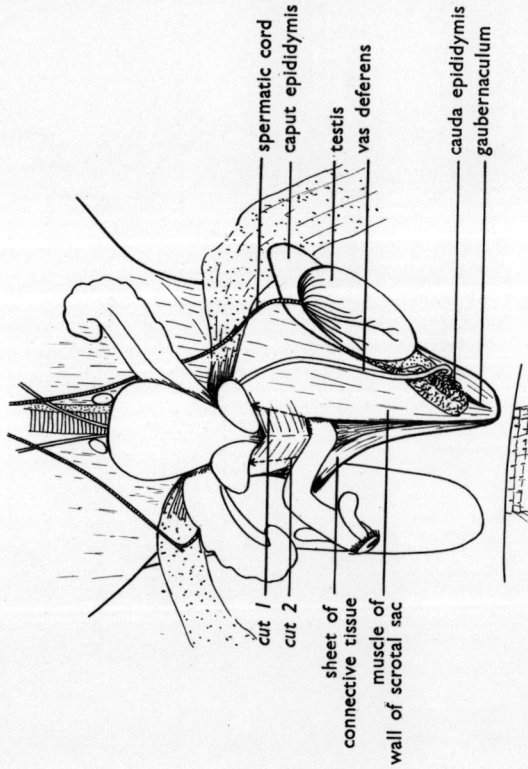

spermatic cord
caput epididymis

testis
vas deferens

cauda epididymis
gaubernaculum

cut 1
cut 2

sheet of
connective tissue
muscle of
wall of scrotal sac

**Fig. 14**

Open the scrotal sac and display the contents as shown.
Cut through the pelvic girdle—cuts 1 and 2.
N.B. Keep the points of the scissors well up.

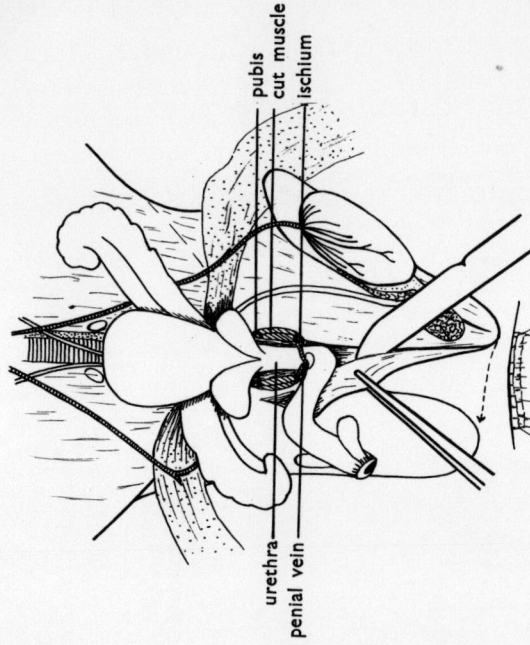

STANDARD × 2

pubis
cut muscle
ischium

urethra
penial vein

**Fig. 15**

Remove the connective tissue from the region between the
scrotal sacs sufficiently to expose the anal canal and the muscles
around the end of the rectum—see Fig. 16.

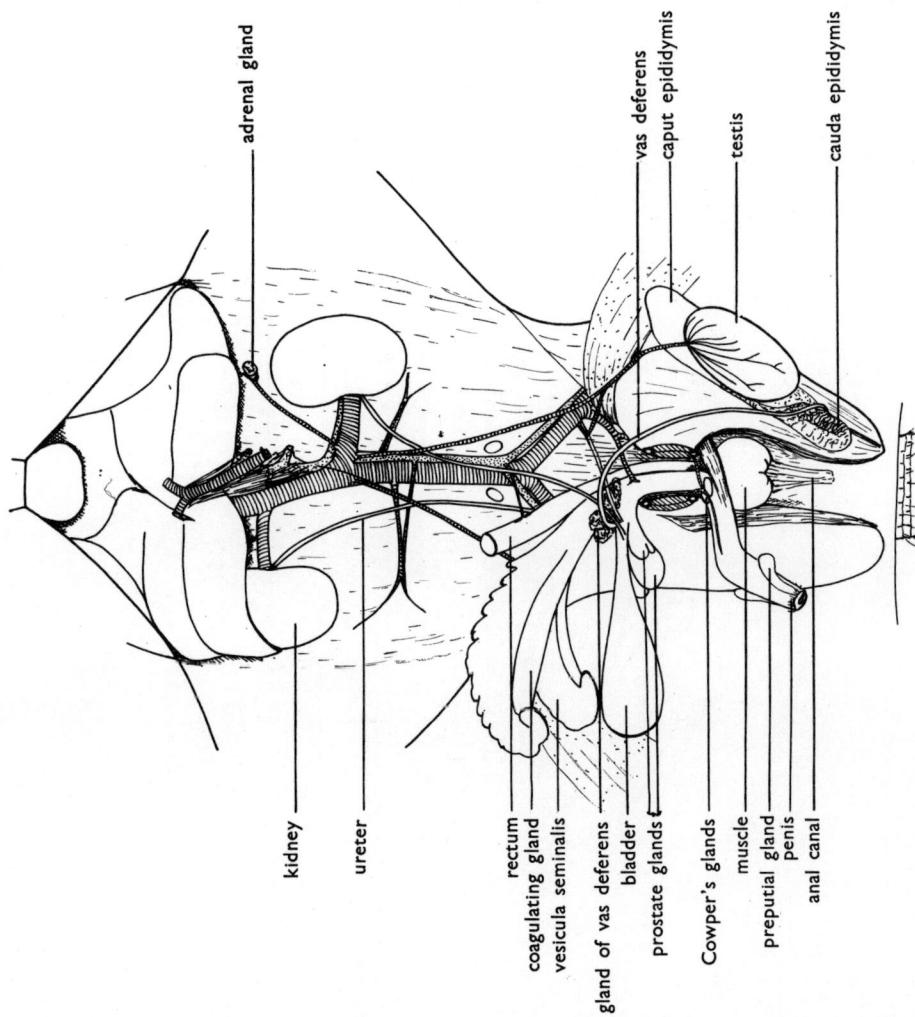

adrenal gland

vas deferens

caput epididymis

testis

cauda epididymis

kidney

ureter

rectum

coagulating gland

vesicula seminalis

gland of vas deferens

bladder

prostate glands

Cowper's glands

muscle

preputial gland

penis

anal canal

**Fig. 16**

Lay the bladder to one side.
Lay the seminal vesicles, coagulating glands and
prostate glands over to the SAME side.
With a needle or fine forceps carefully loosen
the structures from one another till they can be
displayed as shown.
Draw.

STANDARD × 2

## THE ABDOMEN

*(f)* THE FEMALE URINOGENITAL SYSTEM

Before dissecting this system the alimentary canal must be removed as shown in Fig. 12.

There is considerable variation in the amount of fat. A pregnant female as shown in Fig. 18 generally has less fat than a non-pregnant one.

There is also variation in the finer details of the distribution of the blood-vessels which, though they are shown in the following diagrams, need not be cleared till later.

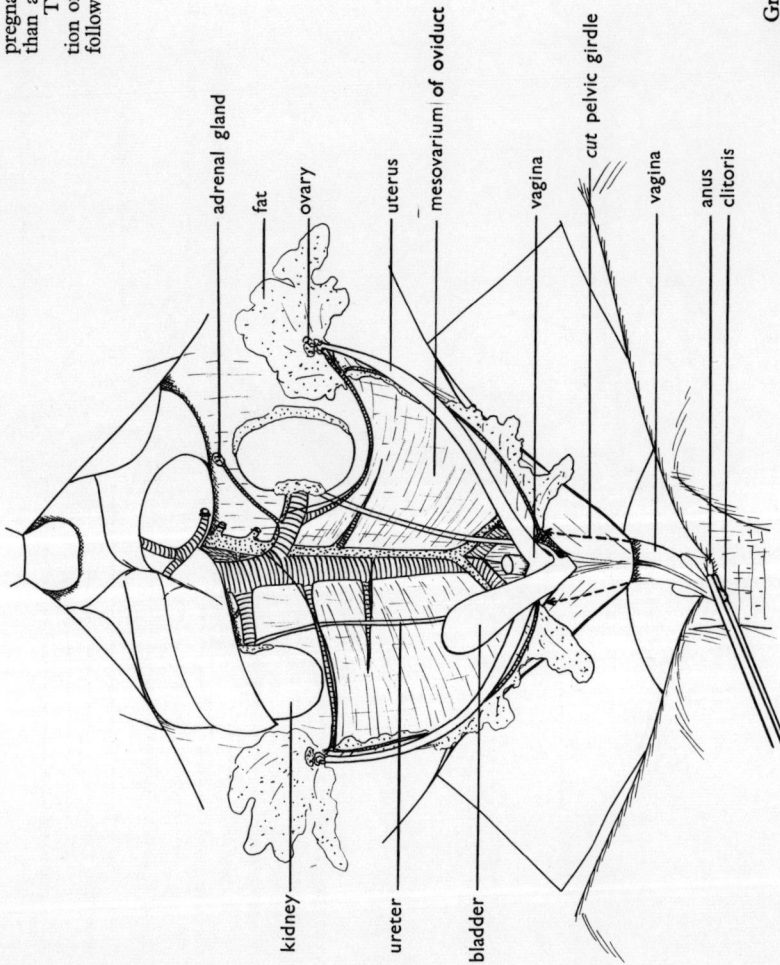

**Fig. 17**

Grip the clitoris and pull it gently so that the urethra is held away from the pelvis. Cut through the pelvic girdle along the lines indicated. Remove the ventral part of the girdle.

Lift the oviducts and remove the mesovarium from them sufficiently to expose the ureters but DO NOT CUT ANY OF THE BLOOD-VESSELS.

If necessary, remove fat from the kidneys and ureters.

Leave the fat around the ovaries and attached to the oviducts, but displace it so that these structures may be observed.

STANDARD × 2

22

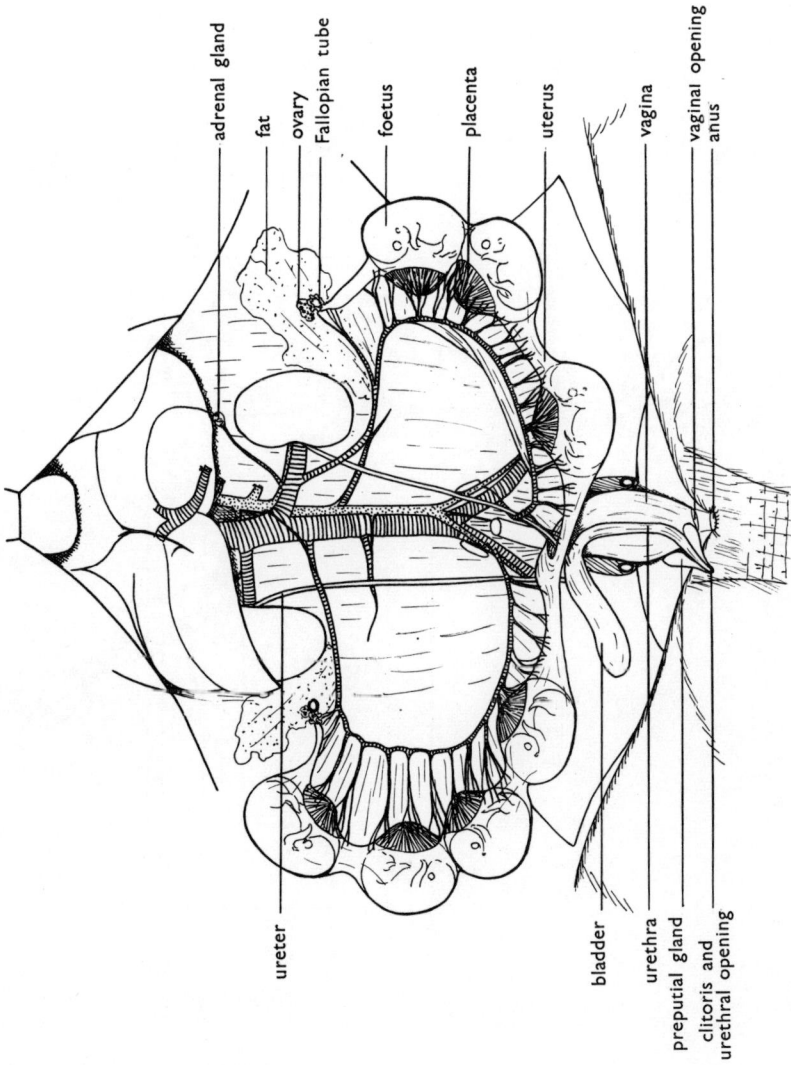

Fallopian tube
uterus
periovarial sac
funnel
ovary

STANDARD × 20

THE FALLOPIAN TUBE

The ovary is enclosed within a thin-walled ovarian sac. The Fallopian tube is very small and much coiled. Its opening from the ovarian sac cannot be seen with the naked eye. It should be examined with the aid of a microscope AFTER completion of the examination of the blood-vessels—see Fig. 19b.

Cut the uterus about half an inch from the Fallopian tube and take out both tube and ovary together. Mount them on a slide, straightening out the coils of the tube as much as possible. Observe and draw.

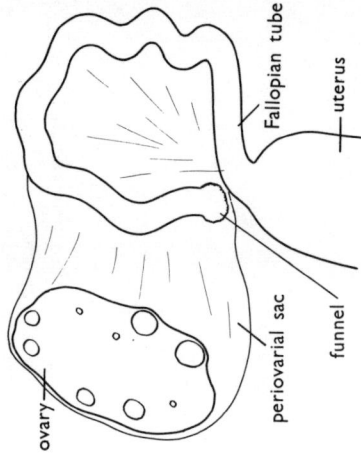

adrenal gland
fat
ovary
Fallopian tube
foetus
placenta
uterus
vagina
vaginal opening
anus

ureter
bladder
urethra
preputial gland
clitoris and urethral opening

STANDARD × 2

Fig. 18

Push back the cut edges of the pelvic girdle. Display the uterus of a pregnant female as shown above. NOTE. In a non-pregnant female the uterus is best left as shown in Fig. 17. Draw.

## THE ABDOMEN

(g) THE BLOOD-VESSELS OF THE ABDOMEN

Before the blood-vessels of the abdomen can be fully displayed the alimentary canal must be removed as shown in Fig. 12 and the pelvic girdle should be cut as shown in Fig. 14 (male) or Fig. 17 (female).

## Fig. 19a. Male

Cut the ureters.

Pin the bladder, seminal vesicles and rectum out of the way as shown.

Remove the RIGHT fat body.

The blood-vessels can be traced through the RIGHT groin by easing away the muscle and connective tissue with forceps. Trim with scissors if necessary.

Clear away the remains of the mesentery and fat to display the aorta and posterior vena cava fully.

NOTES. (1) There is a large anastomosis between the pampiniform plexus and the vesical vein on the LEFT side only.

(2) The positions where the ilio-lumbar and spermatic arteries leave the aorta and the corresponding veins meet the posterior vena cava vary. A common condition in which the left spermatic vessels are branches of the left renal vessels is shown.

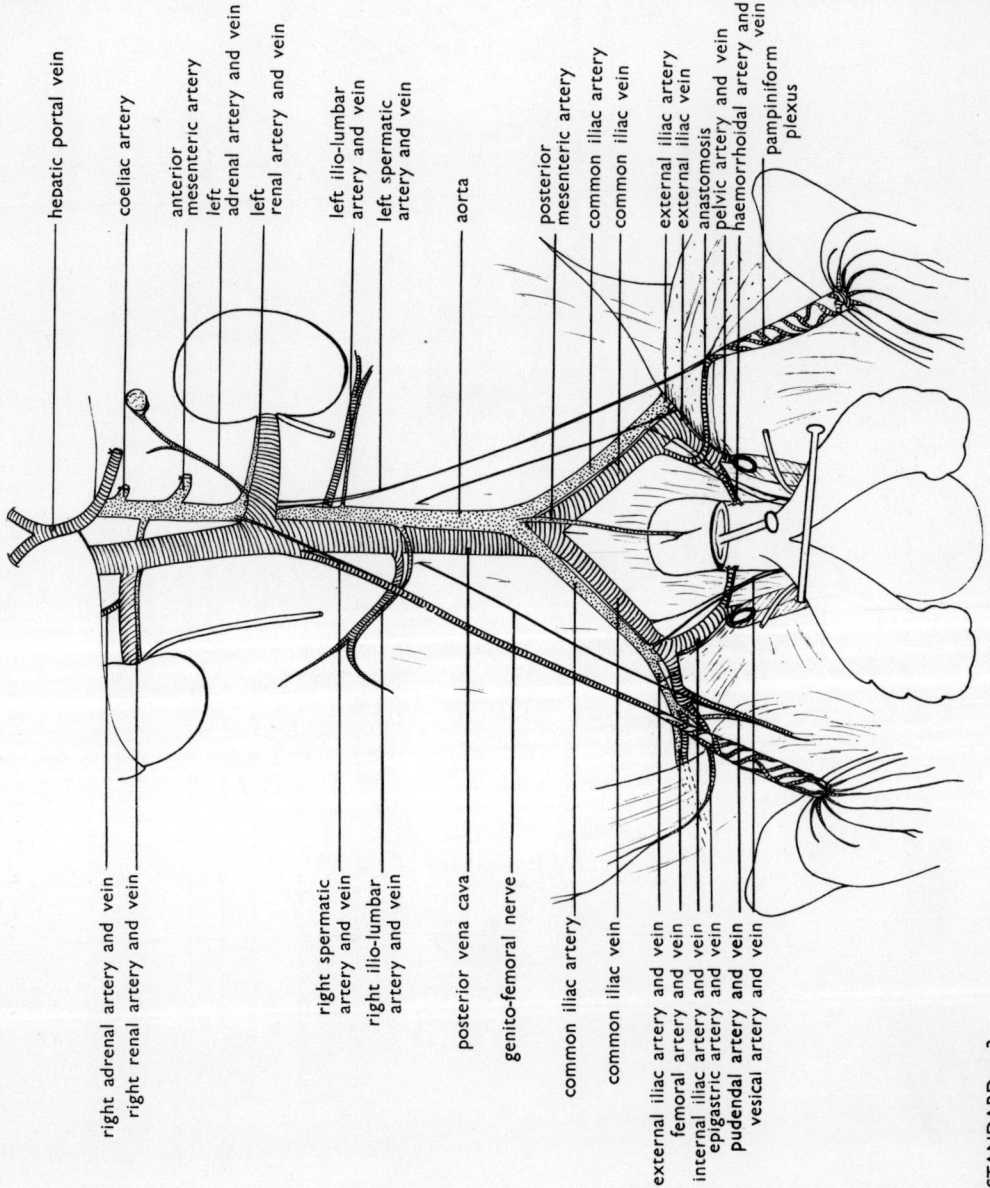

Figure labels:

- hepatic portal vein
- coeliac artery
- anterior mesenteric artery
- left adrenal artery and vein
- left renal artery and vein
- left ilio-lumbar artery and vein
- left spermatic artery and vein
- aorta
- posterior mesenteric artery
- common iliac artery
- common iliac vein
- external iliac artery
- external iliac vein
- anastomosis
- pelvic artery and vein
- haemorrhoidal artery and vein
- pampiniform plexus
- right adrenal artery and vein
- right renal artery and vein
- right spermatic artery and vein
- right ilio-lumbar artery and vein
- posterior vena cava
- genito-femoral nerve
- common iliac artery
- common iliac vein
- external iliac artery and vein
- femoral artery and vein
- internal iliac artery and vein
- epigastric artery and vein
- pudendal artery and vein
- vesical artery and vein

STANDARD × 3

24

THE ABDOMEN

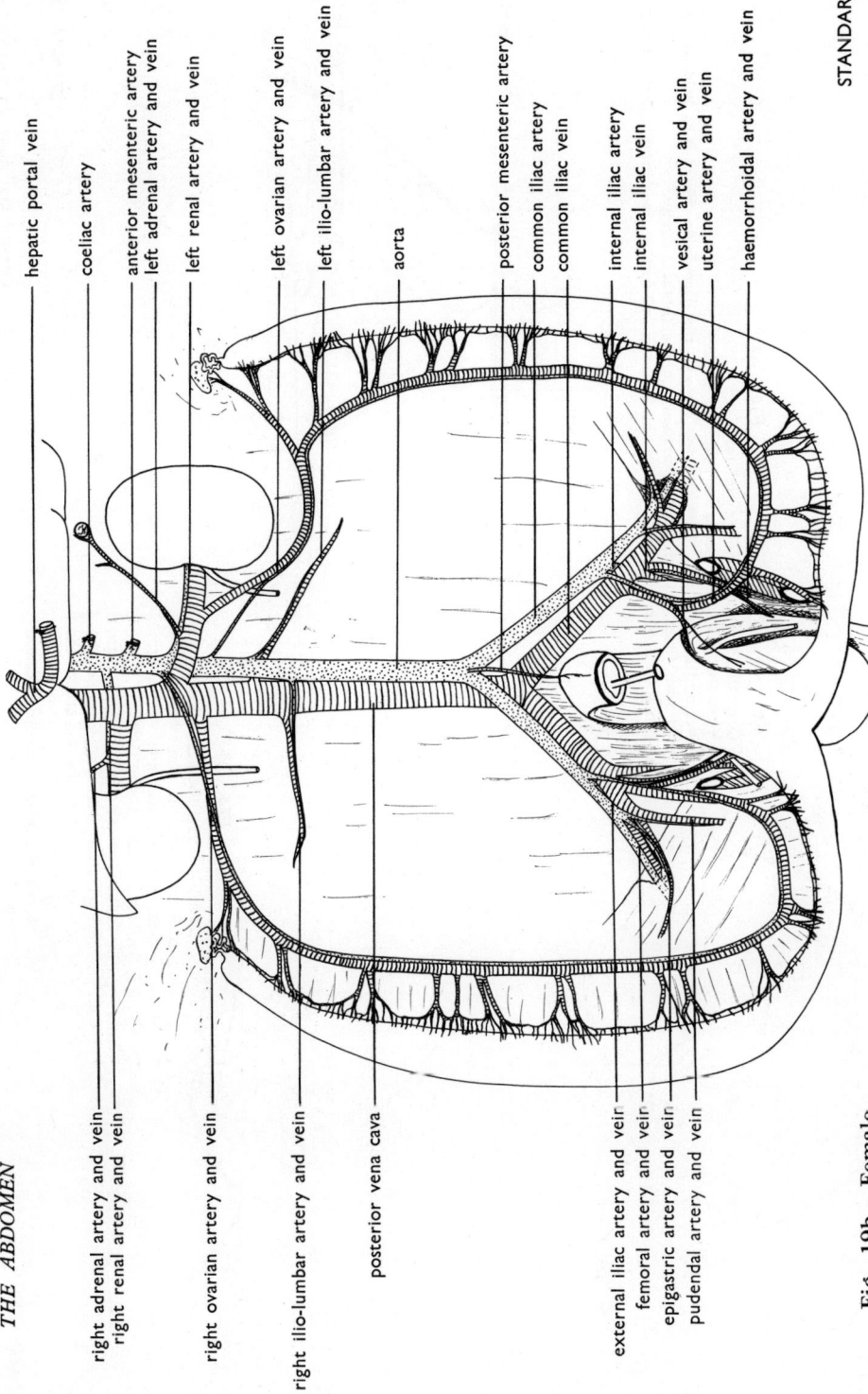

hepatic portal vein

coeliac artery

anterior mesenteric artery
left adrenal artery and vein

left renal artery and vein

left ovarian artery and vein

left ilio-lumbar artery and vein

aorta

posterior mesenteric artery

common iliac artery
common iliac vein

internal iliac artery
internal iliac vein

vesical artery and vein
uterine artery and vein

haemorrhoidal artery and vein

STANDARD × 3

right adrenal artery and vein
right renal artery and vein

right ovarian artery and vein

right ilio-lumbar artery and vein

posterior vena cava

external iliac artery and vein
femoral artery and vein
epigastric artery and vein
pudendal artery and vein

Fig. 19b. Female

Cut the ureters.
Pin the rectum as shown.
Lay the vagina and bladder as shown, pinning if necessary.
The blood-vessels can be traced through the groin by easing away the muscle and connective tissue with forceps. Trim with scissors if necessary.
Clear away the remains of the mesentery and fat to display the aorta and posterior vena cava fully.
NOTES. (1) In some specimens the aorta passes ventral to the left renal vein.
(2) The position of branching of the iliac arteries is very variable. As shown in the diagram, it is not always the same on the two sides of the same rat, but the branches can easily be identified by tracing their distribution.

25

## THE DIAPHRAGM

The diaphragm should be examined on a freshly-killed specimen. It hardens and becomes opaque when preserved. Its elasticity and the negative pressure in the thorax cannot then be observed.

Open the abdominal cavity—see Fig. 4.
Remove the alimentary canal—see Fig. 12.

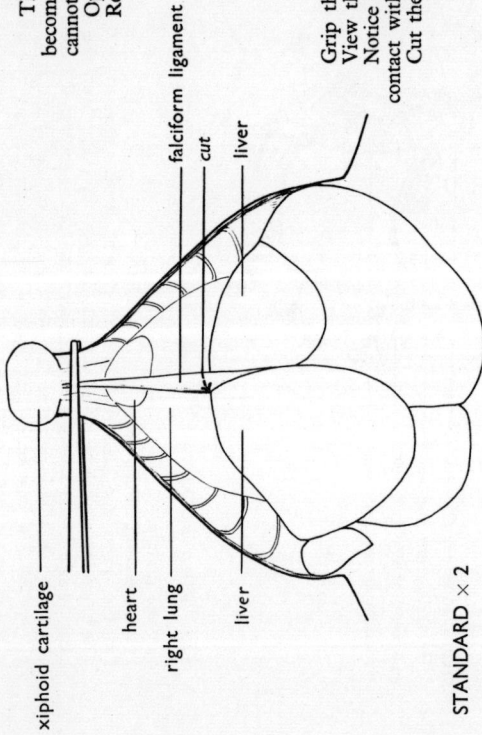

**Fig. 20**

Grip the xiphoid cartilage and raise it.
View the diaphragm from its posterior surface.
Notice the lungs and heart showing through the diaphragm where it is held in close contact with them by the negative pressure in the thoracic cavity.
Cut the falciform ligament so that the liver can fall further away from the diaphragm.

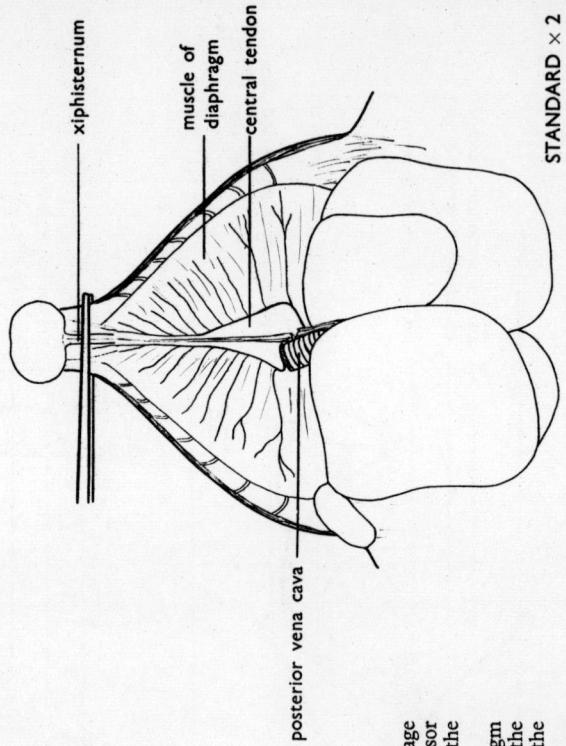

xiphoid cartilage

heart

right lung

liver

falciform ligament

cut

liver

STANDARD × 2

**Fig. 21**

While holding the xiphoid cartilage well up insert the point of a scissor blade through the side wall of the thorax. Make a small slit.

Notice that AT ONCE the diaphragm springs away from the lung on the CUT SIDE ONLY as the air enters the pleural space.

Repeat to perforate the other pleural cavity.

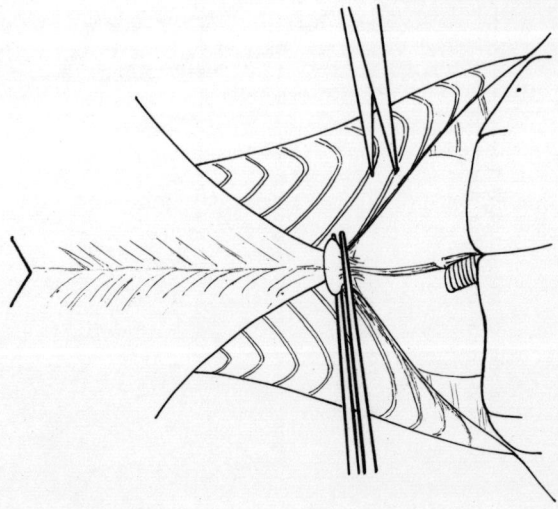

STANDARD × 2

xiphisternum

muscle of diaphragm

central tendon

posterior vena cava

STANDARD × 2

**Fig. 22**  Observe and draw the diaphragm.

## SECTION II—THE THORAX AND NECK

*(a)* OPENING UP THE THORACIC CAVITY

It is not essential to open the abdomen and remove the alimentary canal before dissecting the thorax, but this is usually done because the material in the canal putrifies very rapidly. If the abdomen is left entire it is not necessary to tie back the diaphragm as shown in Fig. 24.

Remember that ANY BLEEDING from the finer vessels which are inevitably cut MUST BE KEPT MOPPED UP with a soft rag. If this is not done the tissues become uniformly stained and the nerves especially are more difficult to identify.

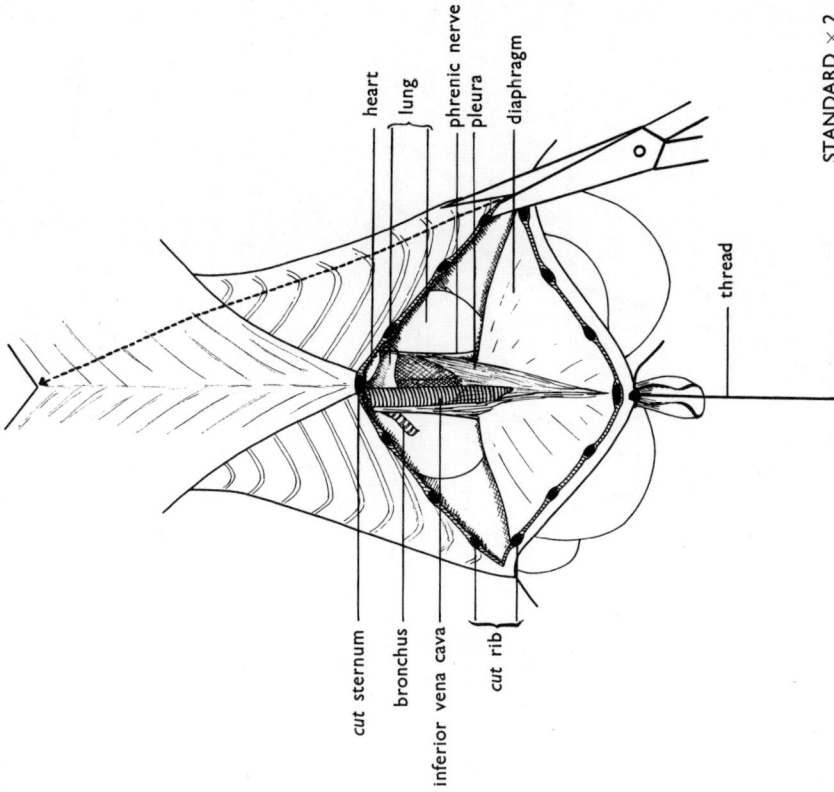

STANDARD × 2

### Fig. 24

Tie a thread round the xiphoid cartilage and attach the other end of the thread to the tail of the rat or to a pin so that the diaphragm is pulled back as shown. NOTE. The pleura surrounding the mediastinum are ruptured by the tension. Cut through the side wall of the thorax along the line indicated—see also Fig. 25.

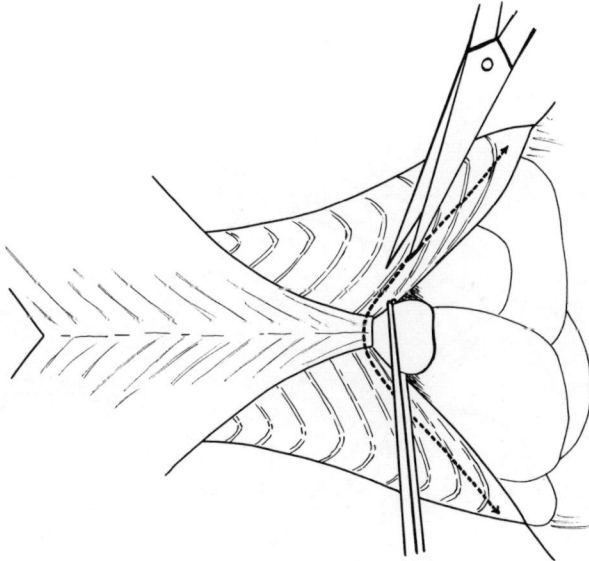

STANDARD × 2

### Fig. 23

Grip the xiphoid cartilage, insert a blade of a pair of scissors through the slit already made (see Fig. 21), and cut through the posterior part of the thoracic wall along the line indicated.

27

*THE THORAX AND NECK*

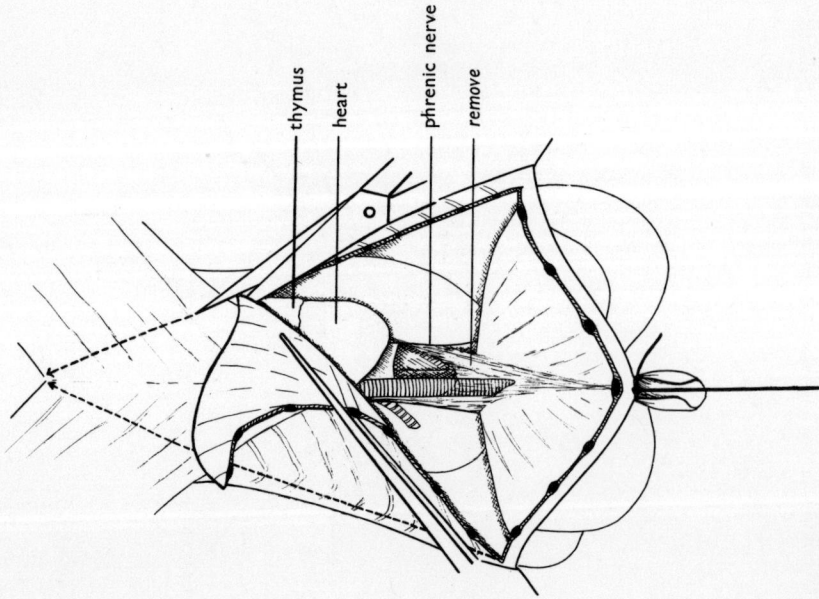

clavicle
first rib
pectoralis muscles
thymus
ventricles of heart
left lung
post-caval lobe of right lung
left phrenic nerve
oesophagus
central tendon of diaphragm

superior lobe of right lung
right auricle of heart
middle lobe of right lung
right phrenic nerve
inferior vena cava
inferior lobe of right lung
diaphragm

STANDARD × 2

### Fig. 26

Observe and draw the contents of the thorax as they appear at this stage.

thymus
heart
phrenic nerve
remove

STANDARD × 2

### Fig. 25

Continue the cut to the apex of the thorax turning the ventral part of the wall aside and pulling it slightly so that there is less danger of cutting the heart. Repeat on the other side to remove the ventral part of the thoracic wall entirely.

Clear away loose parts of the pleura.

NOTE. BE SURE TO CUT THROUGH THE ANTERIOR RIBS AND TO REMOVE THE STERNUM COMPLETELY.

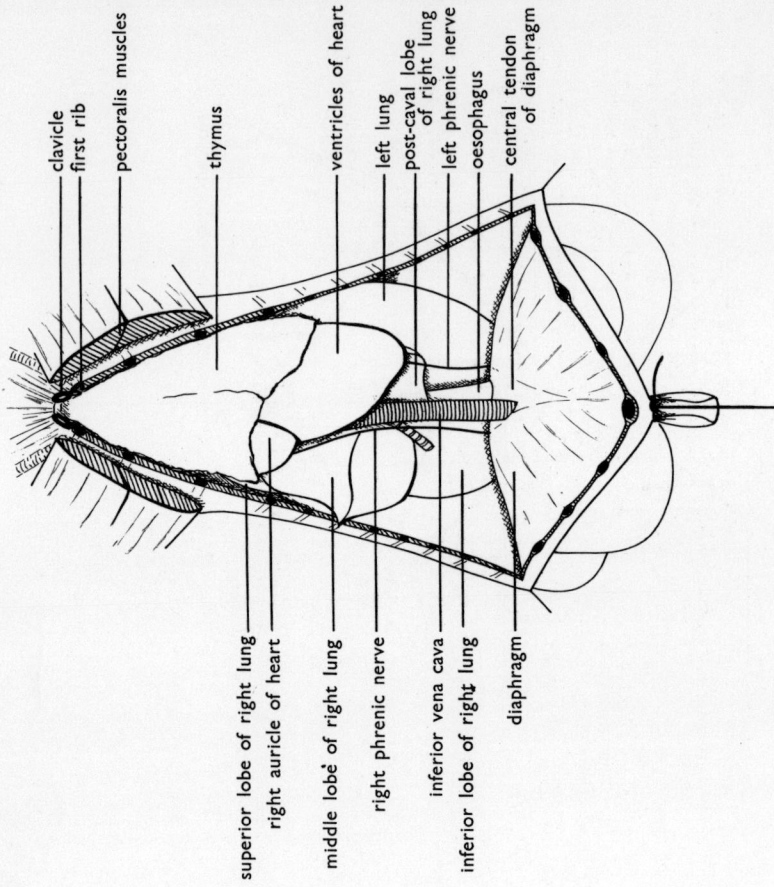

(b) THE HEART AND GREAT BLOOD-VESSELS

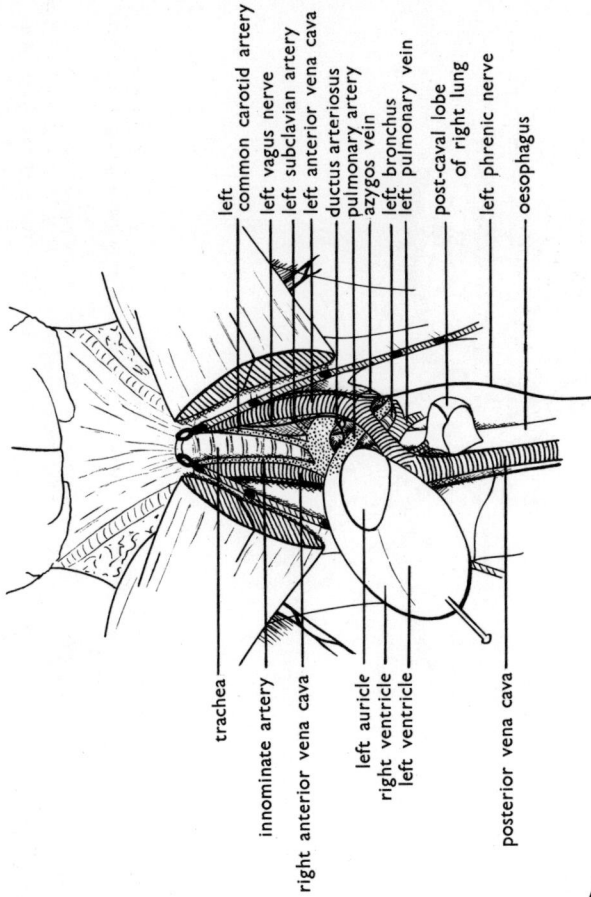

**Fig. 28**

left common carotid artery
left vagus nerve
left subclavian artery
left anterior vena cava
ductus arteriosus
pulmonary artery
azygos vein
left bronchus
left pulmonary vein
post-caval lobe of right lung
left phrenic nerve
oesophagus

trachea
innominate artery
right anterior vena cava
left auricle
right ventricle
left ventricle
posterior vena cava

STANDARD × 2

Pin the heart to the RIGHT of the RAT.
Observe the structures shown in diagram.
Draw.

NOTE. If desired this diagram may be combined with Fig. 34.

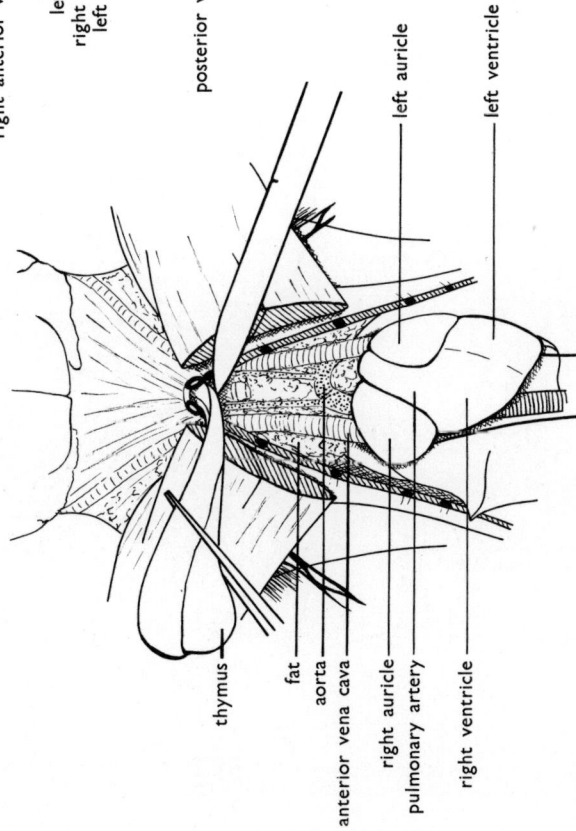

**Fig. 27**

left auricle
left ventricle

thymus
fat
aorta
anterior vena cava
right auricle
pulmonary artery
right ventricle

STANDARD × 2

Remove the thymus gland.
Clear away the fat from around the great vessels.
N.B. WATCH FOR AND DO NOT DESTROY THE PHRENIC AND VAGUS NERVES—see Fig. 28.

(c) THE BLOOD-VESSELS AND NERVES OF THE NECK

The blood-vessels and nerves of the fore-limbs are not usually studied in detail, but their relation to those of the neck and thorax should be noted.

A hand lens may be found useful when looking for the fine nerves of the neck.

N.B. MOP UP ALL CAPILLARY BLEEDING AT ONCE WITH A SOFT CLOTH.

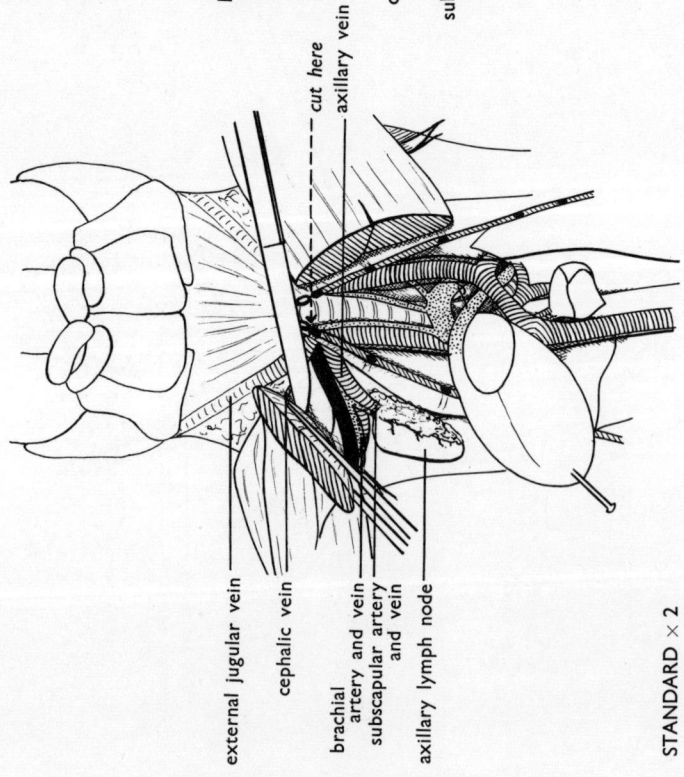

external jugular vein
cephalic vein
brachial artery and vein
subscapular artery and vein
axillary lymph node
cut here
axillary vein

STANDARD × 2

Fig. 29

Lift the pectoralis muscles and carefully clear them from the axillary vessels and nerves.

Keep the blocks of muscle entire and cut each of them as close as possible to its insertion—see Fig. 30.

Cut between the clavicle and the first rib to trace the connection between the axillary vein and the anterior vena cava, i.e. the very short subclavian vein. Push the rib aside and trim if necessary.

N.B. BE CAREFUL NOT TO CUT THE PHRENIC NERVE.

Repeat on the other side.

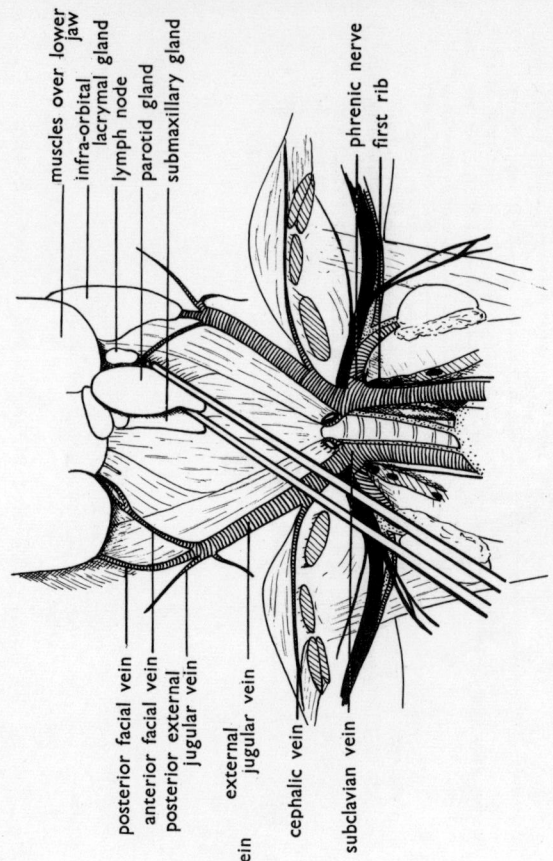

muscles over lower jaw
infra-orbital lacrymal gland
lymph node
parotid gland
submaxillary gland
phrenic nerve
first rib
posterior facial vein
anterior facial vein
posterior external jugular vein
external jugular vein
cephalic vein
subclavian vein

STANDARD × 2

Fig. 30

Clear away any fat and connective tissue that may be masking the external jugular veins.

Lift aside the salivary glands and trace the anterior facial vein.

Remove the glands and the lymph nodes.

Remove the infra-orbital lacrymal gland to expose the posterior facial vein.

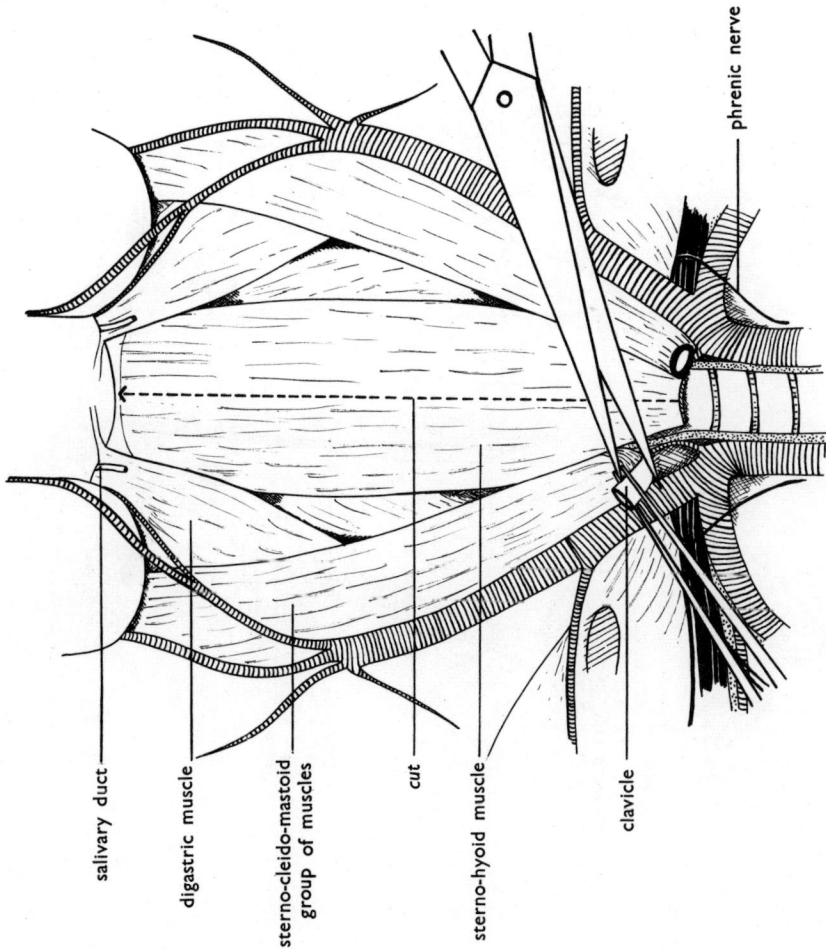

salivary duct

digastric muscle

sterno-cleido-mastoid group of muscles

cut

sterno-hyoid muscle

clavicle

phrenic nerve

STANDARD × 4

**Fig. 31**

Lift the clavicle and trim it as close to the external jugular vein as possible.

Cut between the blocks of sterno-hyoid muscle along the line indicated.

N.B. Be careful not to damage the trachea and larynx which lie immediately underneath these muscles.

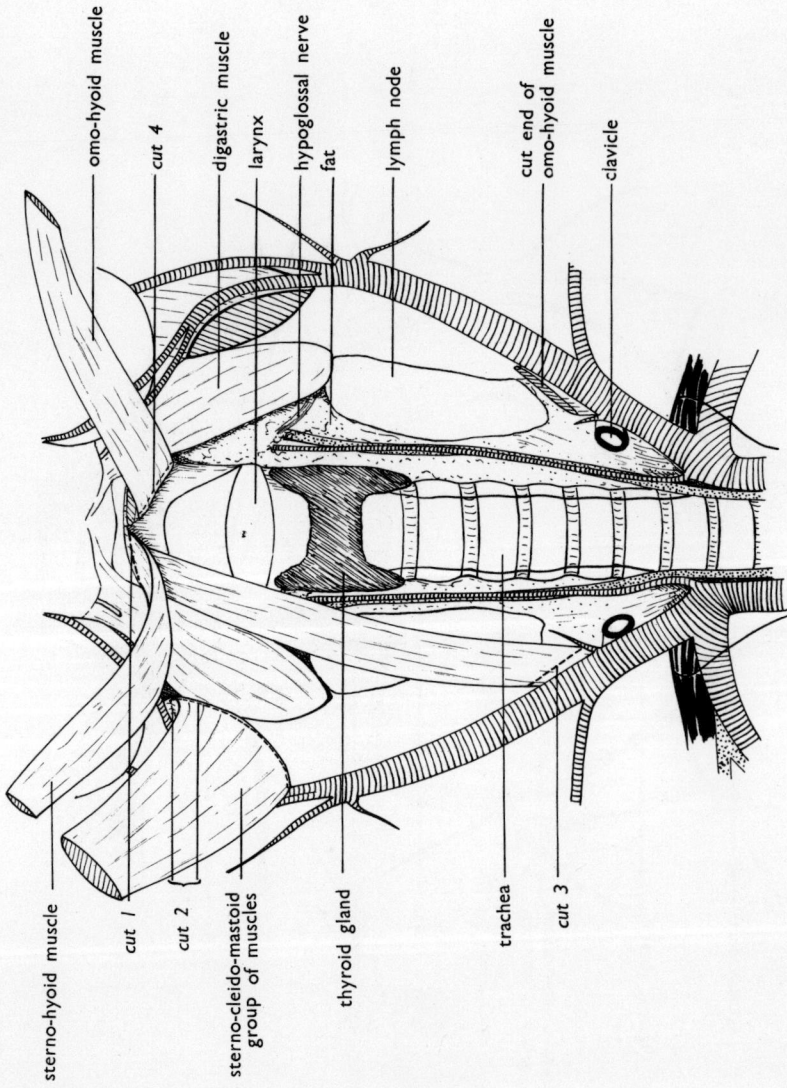

**Fig. 32**

Loosen and cut the sterno-hyoid, sterno-cleido-mastoid and omo-hyoid muscles as indicated—cuts 1, 2, 3, and 4.

STANDARD × 4

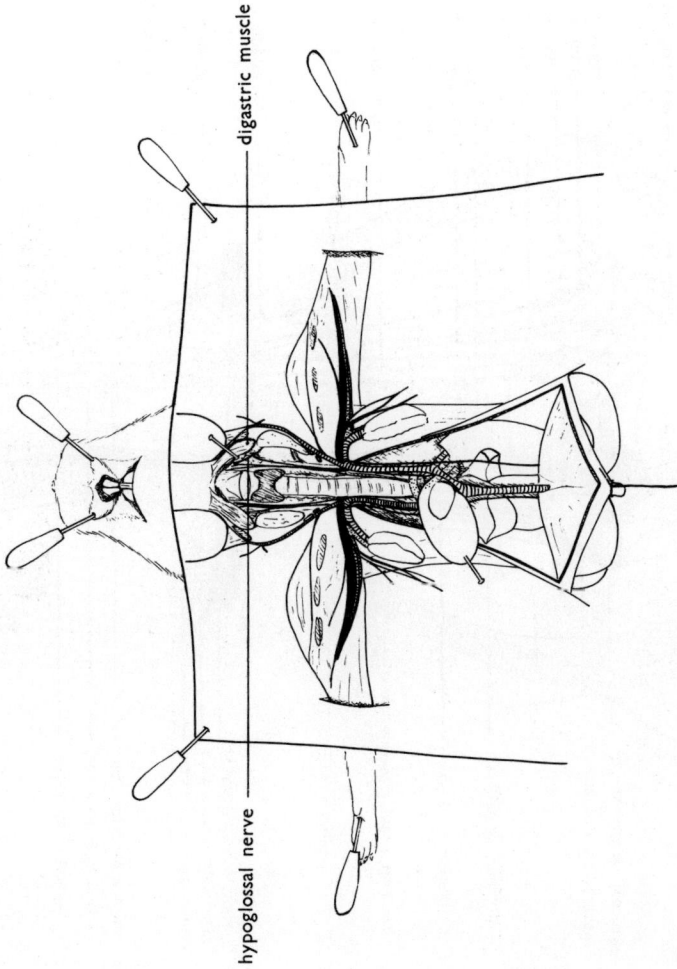

digastric muscle

hypoglossal nerve

**Fig. 33**

Place pins through the upper lips as shown. This arches the neck slightly and makes the display of the nerves and blood-vessels of the neck easier.

Remove some of the fat carefully until the hypoglossal nerve can be identified.

Pin aside the posterior part of the digastric muscle carefully avoiding the nerve.

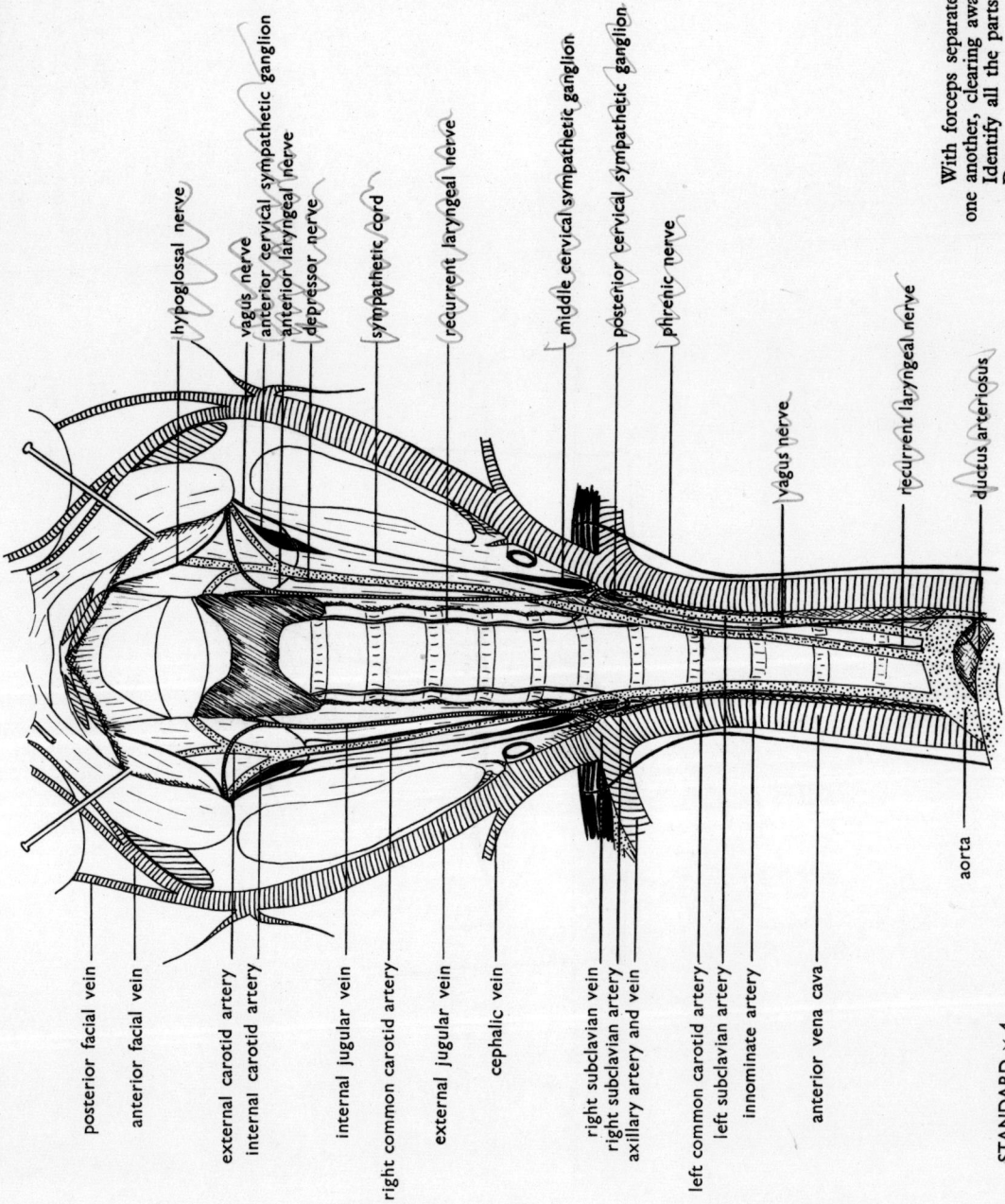

hypoglossal nerve

vagus nerve
anterior cervical sympathetic ganglion
anterior laryngeal nerve
depressor nerve

sympathetic cord

recurrent laryngeal nerve

middle cervical sympathetic ganglion
posterior cervical sympathetic ganglion
phrenic nerve

vagus nerve

recurrent laryngeal nerve
ductus arteriosus

aorta

posterior facial vein
anterior facial vein

external carotid artery
internal carotid artery

internal jugular vein
right common carotid artery
external jugular vein

cephalic vein

right subclavian vein
right subclavian artery
axillary artery and vein

left common carotid artery
left subclavian artery
innominate artery

anterior vena cava

STANDARD × 4

**Fig. 34**

With forceps separate the blood-vessels and nerves from
one another, clearing away fat where necessary.
Identify all the parts shown in diagram.
Draw.

(d) EXAMINATION OF THE HEART AND LUNGS ISOLATED

A more detailed study of the heart and lungs may be performed by removing them from the body and dissecting them separately.

When fresh, the isolated heart-lung preparation is soft and difficult to handle. A day or more in formalin makes the following parts of the dissection much easier.

Loosen the trachea and oesophagus from the back of the neck.

Cut through the pharynx immediately anterior to the larynx.

Cut the venae cavae, the innominate, left common carotid and left subclavian arteries at the points marked X.

NOTE. There is no need to ligature these blood-vessels.

Cut the oesophagus close to the diaphragm.

The aorta and azygos vein can then be seen and cut also close to the diaphragm.

Loosen the oesophagus, aorta and azygos vein from the back of the thorax.

Lift out the heart, lungs and oesophagus together.

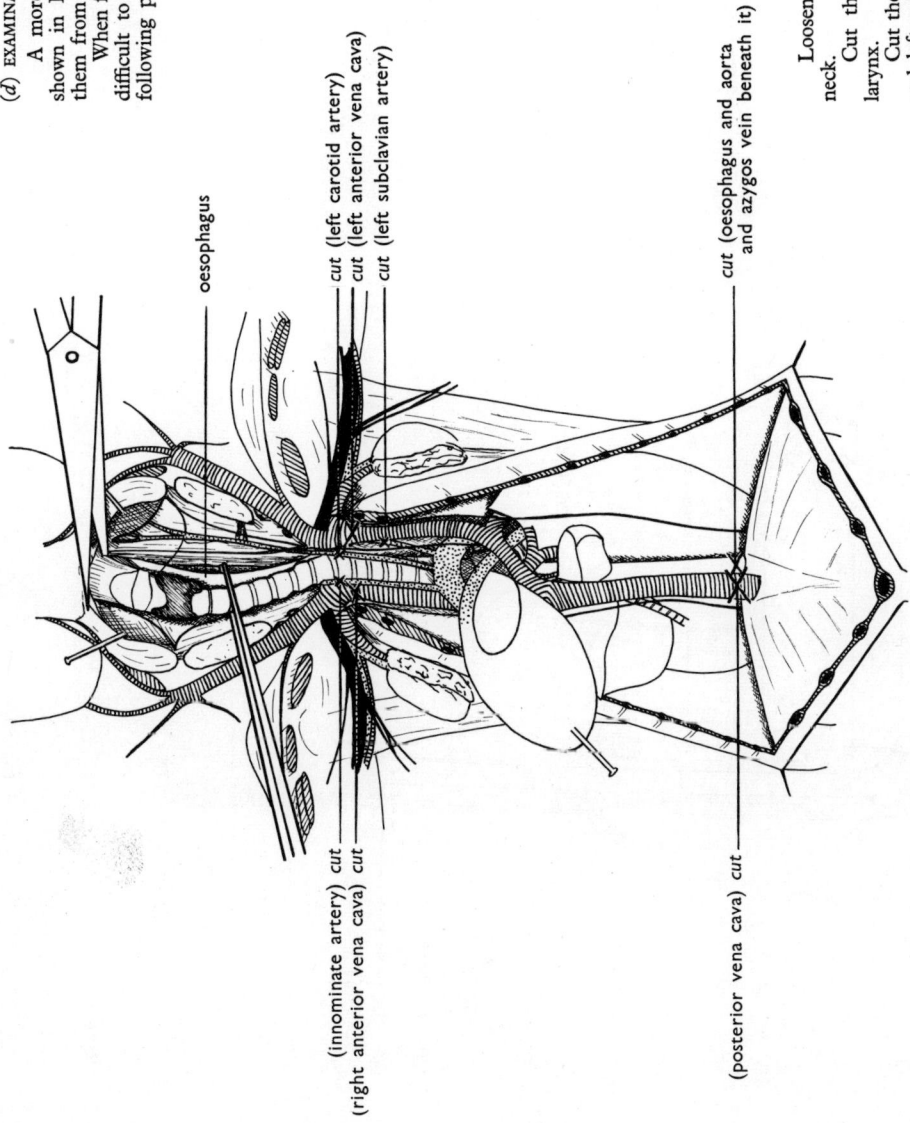

Fig. 35

oesophagus

cut (left carotid artery)
cut (left anterior vena cava)
cut (left subclavian artery)

(innominate artery) cut
(right anterior vena cava) cut

cut (oesophagus and aorta and azygos vein beneath it)

(posterior vena cava) cut

STANDARD × 2

35

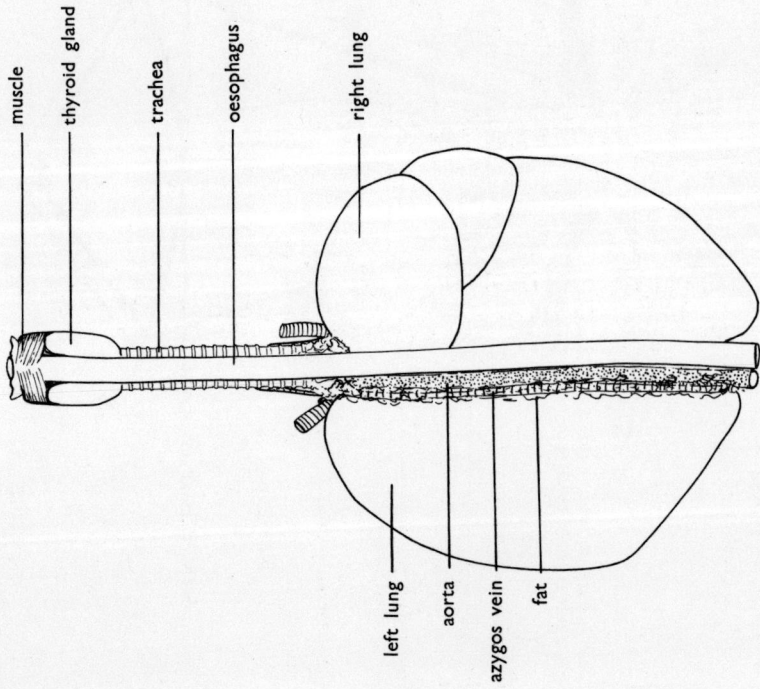

**Fig. 37**

Starting at the posterior end, separate the oesophagus from the trachea, holding the preparation as shown.

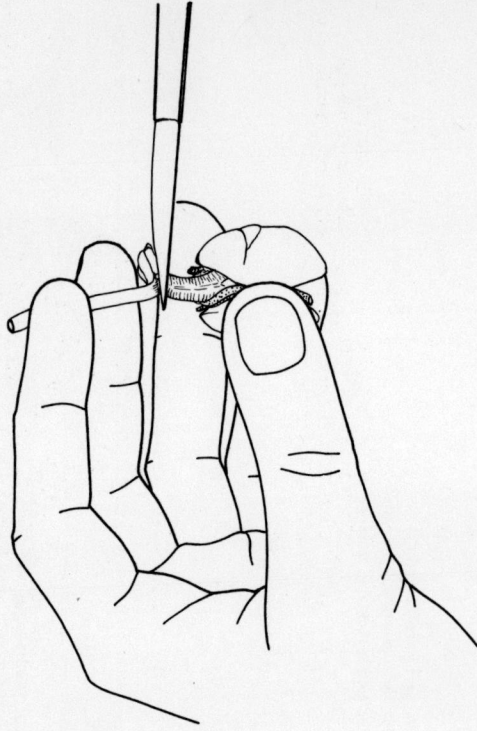

muscle

thyroid gland

trachea

oesophagus

right lung

left lung

aorta

azygos vein

fat

STANDARD × 3

**Fig. 36**

Observe the parts now isolated in dorsal view. Note the relationship of the oesophagus to the larynx and trachea.

cut

**Fig. 39**

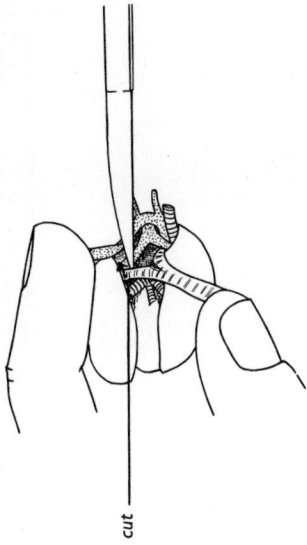

Separate the bronchi from the pulmonary arteries.
Cut through each pulmonary vein, bronchus and pulmonary artery as indicated to remove the lungs, but leave as much as possible of the blood-vessels.

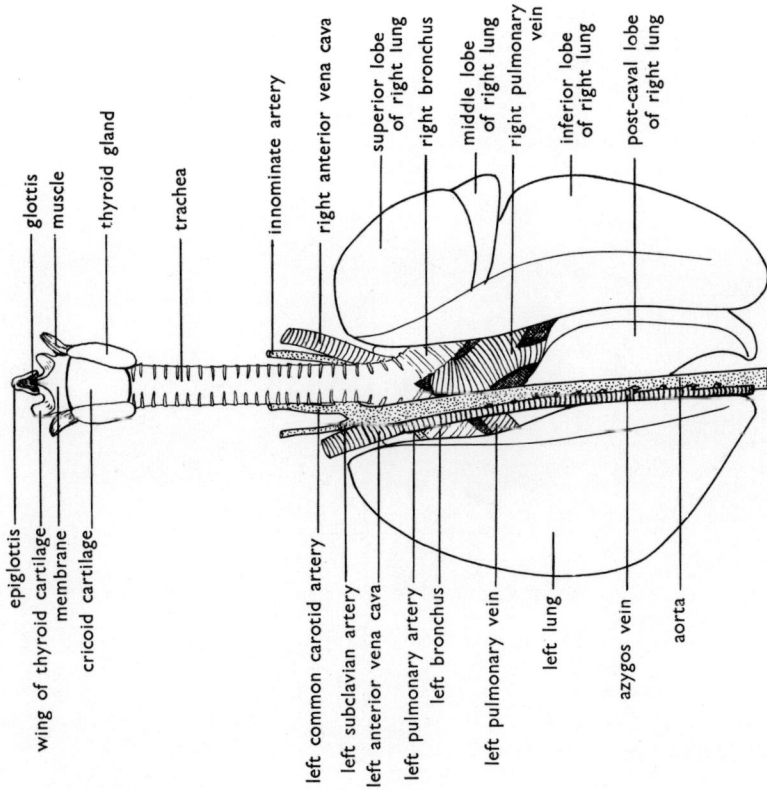

pulmonary artery
right auricle
vena cava entering right auricle
right ventricle
left ventricle

aorta
ductus arteriosus
pulmonary vein entering left auricle
left auricle

STANDARD × 3

**Fig. 40**

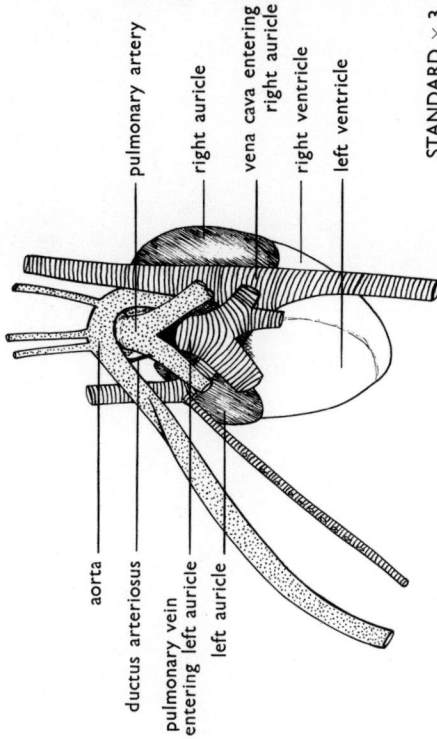

Lay aside the aorta and azygos vein.
Study the dorsal view of the heart and the relation of the blood-vessels to it.
Draw.

epiglottis
glottis
muscle
wing of thyroid cartilage
membrane
thyroid gland
cricoid cartilage
trachea

innominate artery
left common carotid artery
right anterior vena cava
left subclavian artery
superior lobe of right lung
left anterior vena cava
right bronchus
left pulmonary artery
middle lobe of right lung
left bronchus
right pulmonary vein
left pulmonary vein
inferior lobe of right lung
left lung
post-caval lobe of right lung
azygos vein
aorta

STANDARD × 3

**Fig. 38**

Clear any fat from the bronchi and blood-vessels.
Identify the parts shown.
Draw.

## SECTION III—THE BRAIN

Nervous tissue is very soft and has very little elasticity. Even after 'hardening' with formalin it is much softer and more easily cut than other tissues. It is therefore very easily damaged by any slip of the instruments and the removal of the brain requires much care and patience. The skull must be cut away in VERY SMALL PIECES and the pressure on the instruments must be fully under control all the time.

A hand lens will be found useful when examining the cranial nerves.

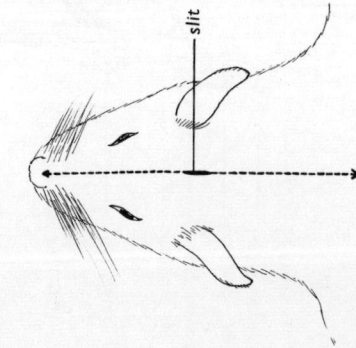

**Fig. 41**

Hold the rat dorsal side uppermost.
Make a small slit in the skin between the pinnae.
Continue the slit forwards to the snout and backwards to the level of the fore-limbs.

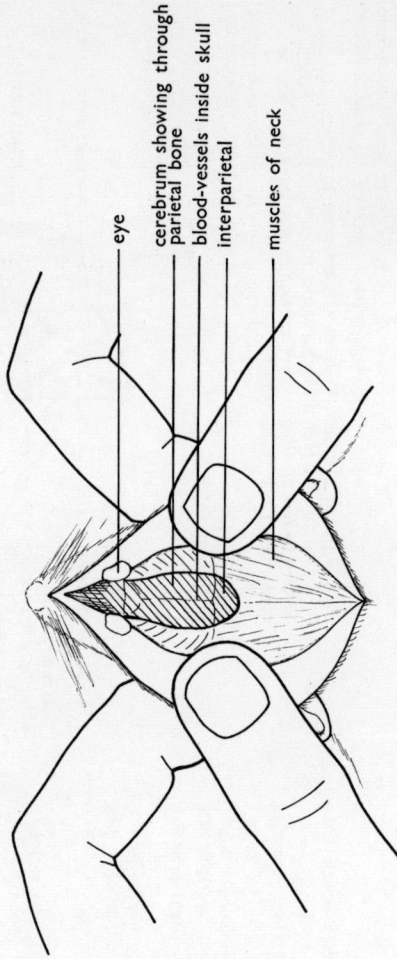

eye
cerebrum showing through parietal bone
blood-vessels inside skull
interparietal
muscles of neck

slit

**Fig. 42**

Pull aside the skin, using the thumb and forefinger of each hand as shown.
Notice the brain showing through the roof of the skull.

38

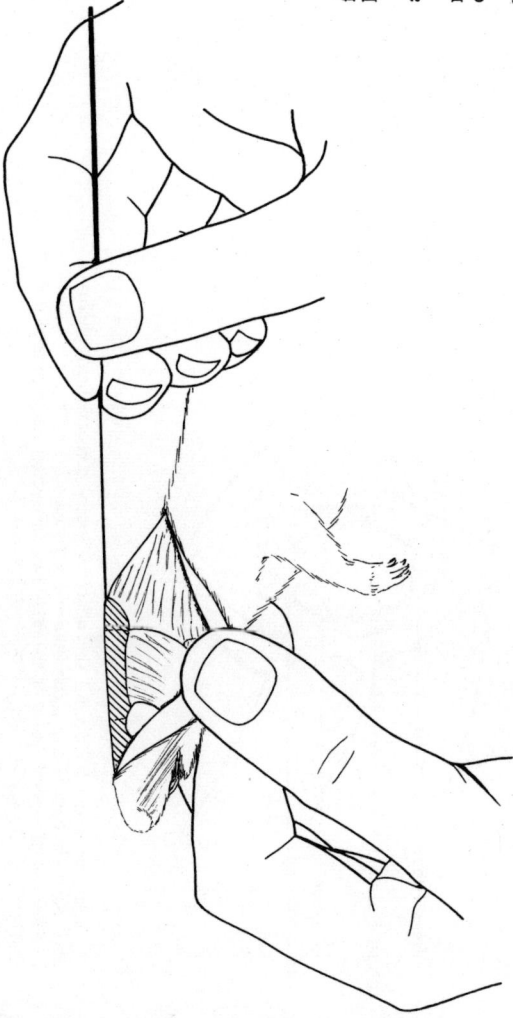

## Fig. 43

Grip the head of the rat with the thumb and second finger and support the chin with the first finger of the left hand. The free part of the skin helps to give a good grip.

Hold a scalpel level with the back of the skull as shown and pierce the interparietal bone.

NOTE. It is very important to MAINTAIN THE HORIZONTAL POSITION OF THE SCALPEL. Any tilting will either cause piercing of the brain or failure to perforate the skull.

The entry of the scalpel point causes the interparietal bone to crack away along the sutures with the parietals and squamosals.

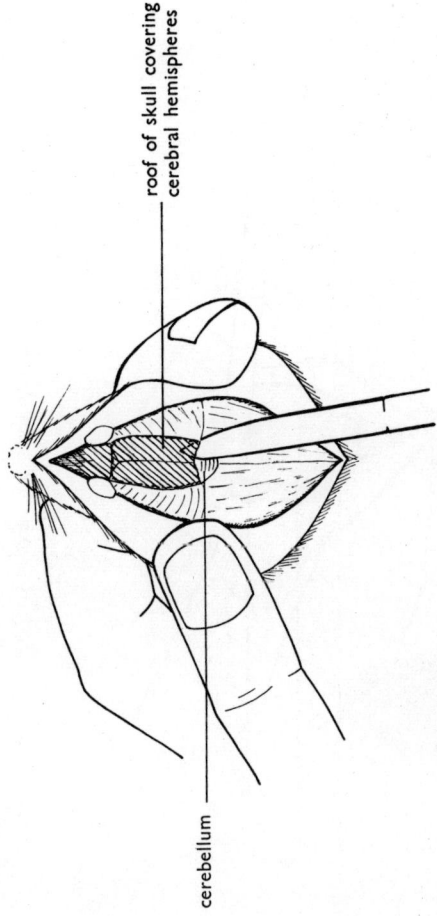

## Fig. 44

Notice the exposed part of the cerebellum.

With a scalpel chip away the roof of the skull over the area indicated by the dotted lines.

roof of skull covering cerebral hemispheres

cerebellum

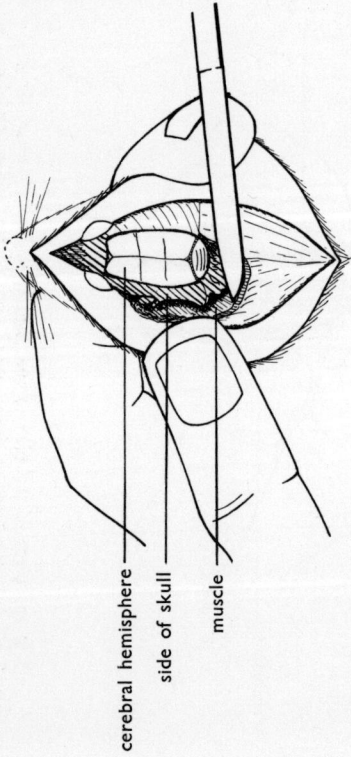

**Fig. 45**

Scrape aside the muscles to expose the sides and posterior part of the skull.

cerebral hemisphere
side of skull
muscle

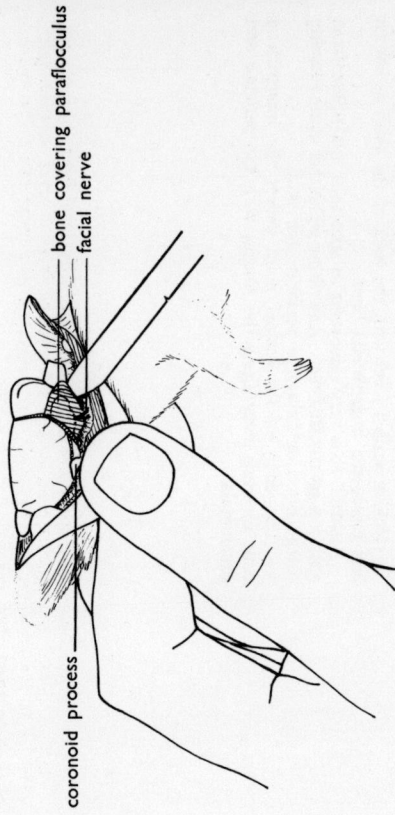

**Fig. 47**

Cut through the spinal cord.
Cut UNDER THE SKULL as indicated, cutting the posterior cranial nerves in the process.
Continue till the facial nerves are cut.

bone covering paraflocculus
facial nerve
coronoid process

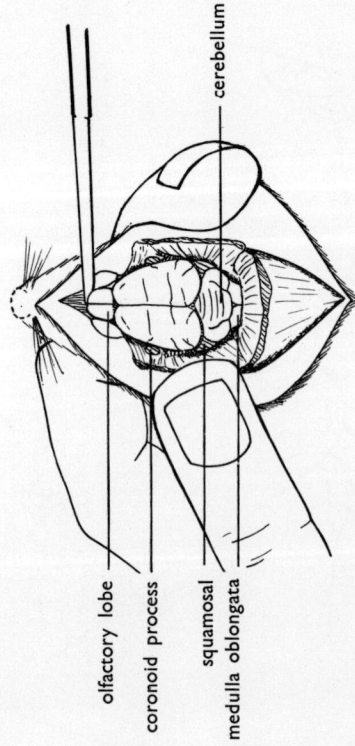

**Fig. 46**

Chip away the bone until the olfactory lobes, cerebral hemispheres and the main part of the cerebellum are exposed.
Remove the dorsal parts of the atlas and axis vertebrae to expose the first part of the spinal cord.
Cut under the olfactory lobes.

cerebellum
olfactory lobe
coronoid process
squamosal
medulla oblongata

40

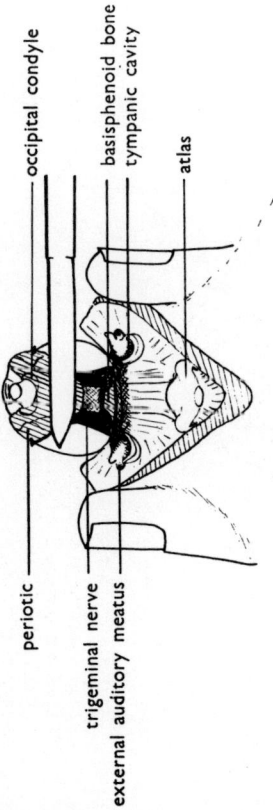

bone covering paraflocculus

**Fig. 50**

Grip the bone with forceps and cut it away little by little from the auditory region. Leave the occipital condyle as long as possible as it gives the best grip. N.B. TRY NOT TO TOUCH OR GRIP THE NERVOUS TISSUE WITH THE INSTRUMENTS. Cut away VERY SMALL PIECES at a time.
BE VERY CAREFUL NOT TO DAMAGE THE PARAFLOCCULUS which is almost entirely surrounded by bone.
NOTE. The bone can be felt as it is hard and grates against the forceps.
The brain may be supported on the dissecting board or held with the fingers but NOT with instruments.

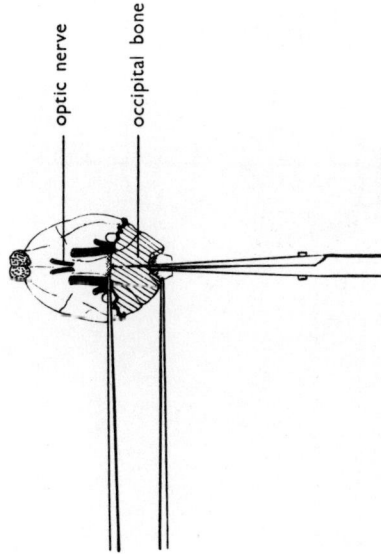

occipital condyle
basisphenoid bone
tympanic cavity
atlas
periotic
trigeminal nerve
**external auditory meatus**

**Fig. 48**

Change the grip and the position of the scalpel. Prise the posterior part of the base of the skull upwards. This breaks the suture between the occipital and basisphenoid bones and also between the tympanic bulla and the periotic.
Notice the large trigeminal nerves. Cut these nerves as close as possible to the foramina through which they leave the skull.
Cut the optic nerves also—see Fig. 49.
Remove the brain from the head.

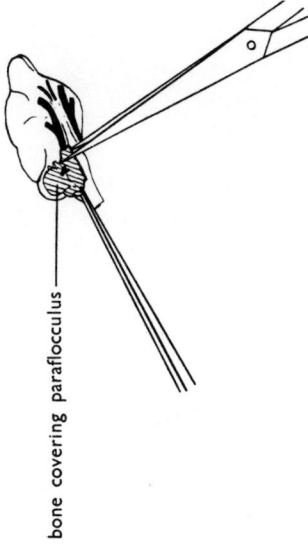

optic nerve
occipital bone

**Fig. 49**

Grip the piece of the base of the skull which is still attached to the brain. Using scissors, cut through the occipital bone in the mid-ventral line.

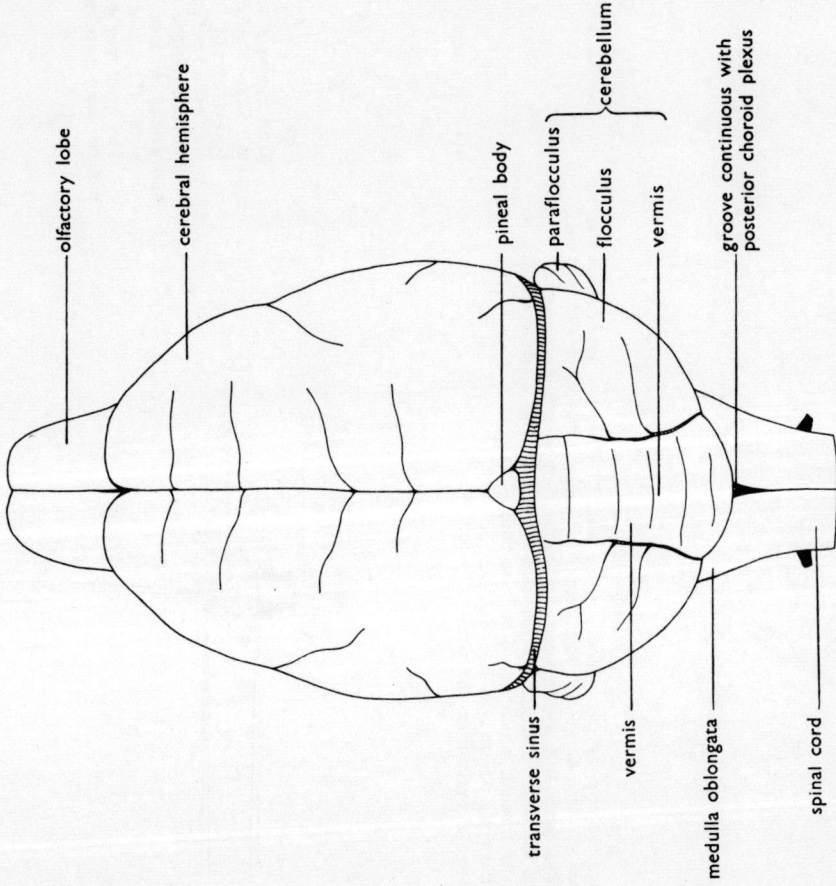

olfactory lobe

cerebral hemisphere

pineal body

paraflocculus

flocculus

vermis

cerebellum

groove continuous with
posterior choroid plexus

transverse sinus

vermis

medulla oblongata

spinal cord

STANDARD × 5

**Fig. 51**

Examine the brain in dorsal view. Draw.

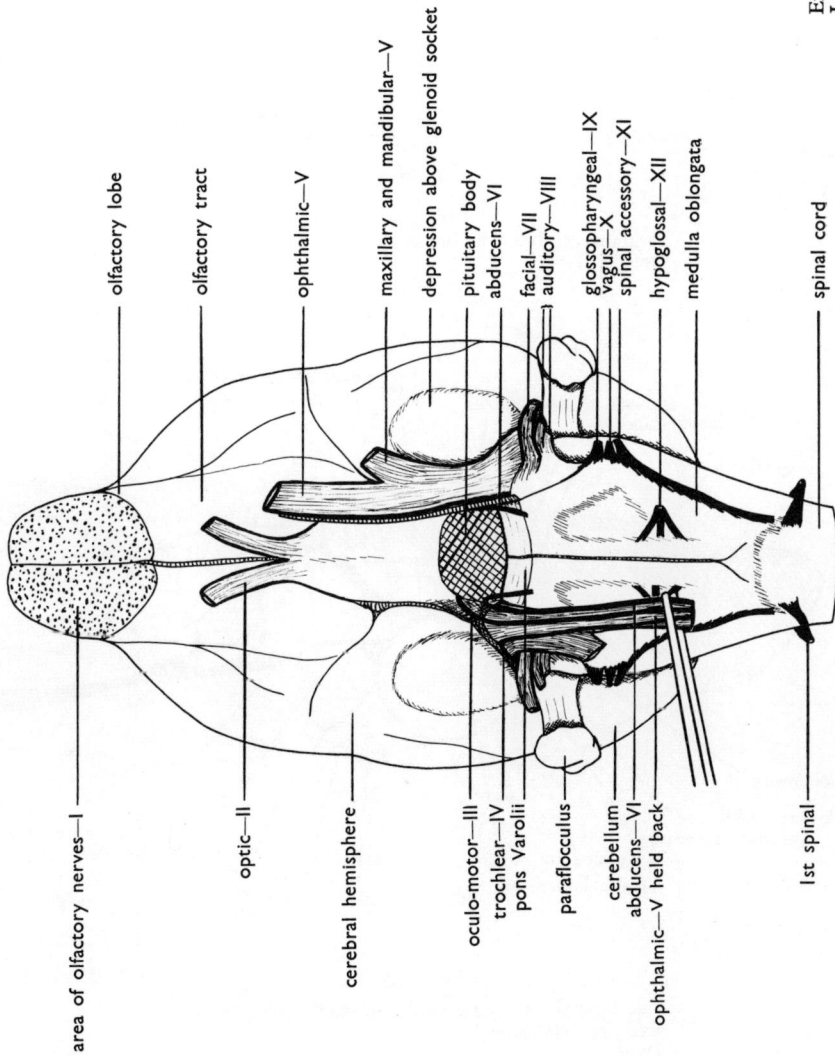

area of olfactory nerves—I

olfactory lobe

olfactory tract

optic—II

ophthalmic—V

cerebral hemisphere

maxillary and mandibular—V

depression above glenoid socket

pituitary body

oculo-motor—III
trochlear—IV
pons Varolii

abducens—VI

facial—VII
auditory—VIII

paraflocculus

glossopharyngeal—IX
vagus—X
spinal accessory—XI

cerebellum
abducens—VI
ophthalmic—V held back

hypoglossal—XII

medulla oblongata

1st spinal

spinal cord

**Fig. 52**

Examine the brain in ventral view.
Loosen the trigeminal nerve from the ventral surface of
the fore-brain and turn it back as shown. Look for the
oculomotor, trochlear and abducens nerves which lie close to
the trigeminal and are turned back with it.
Holding the trigeminal nerve as shown, draw.
NOTE. Because of the amount of labelling in this diagram
the word 'nerve' has been omitted throughout.

STANDARD × 5

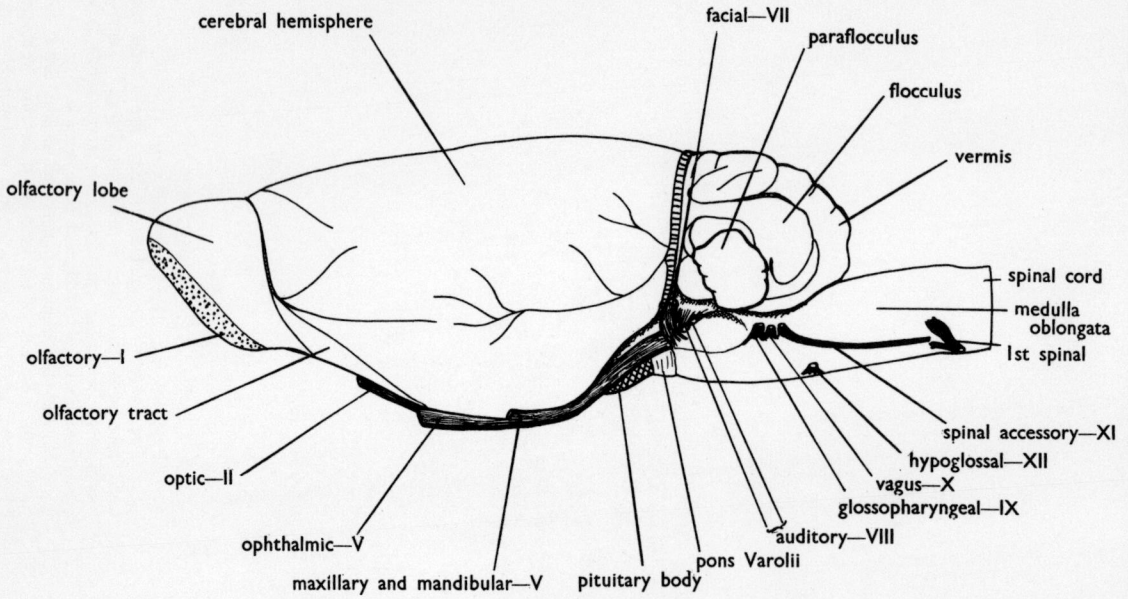

STANDARD × 5

**Fig. 53**
Examine the brain in lateral view.
Draw.

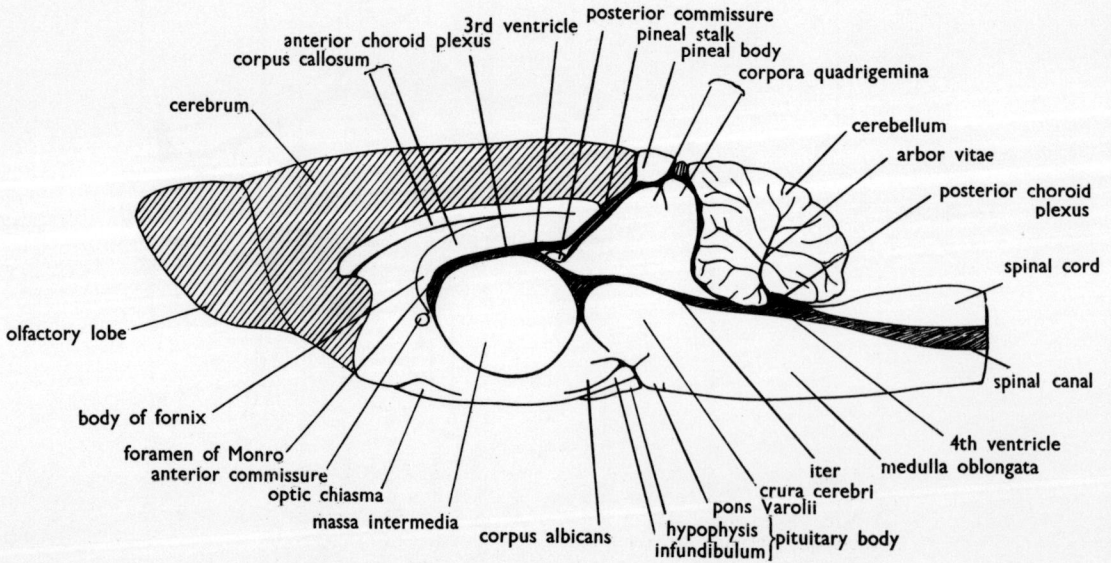

STANDARD × 5

**Fig. 54**
Cut through the brain in the median sagittal plane.
Examine the section.
Draw.

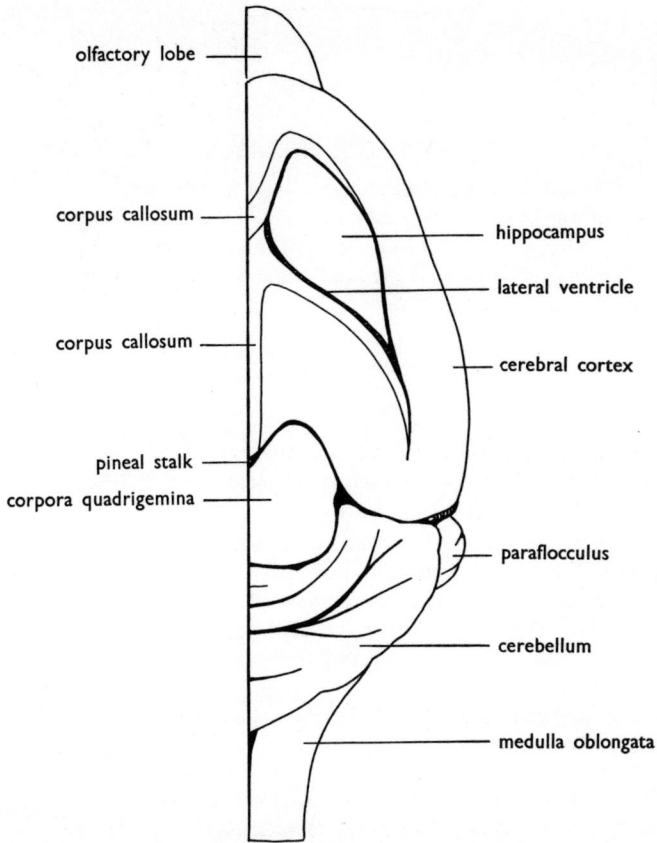

olfactory lobe

corpus callosum

hippocampus

lateral ventricle

corpus callosum

cerebral cortex

pineal stalk

corpora quadrigemina

paraflocculus

cerebellum

medulla oblongata

STANDARD × 5

**Fig. 55**

Using one-half of the brain, slice away the dorsal parts little by little until the hippocampus can be seen clearly.

N.B. Keep the cut level through the olfactory lobe, cerebral hemisphere, corpora quadrigemina and cerebellum.

The level required is about one-third down from the dorsal surface.

Draw.

# APPENDIX—THE SKELETON

The skeleton can easily be examined by boiling a freshly-killed, eviscerated rat, and separating the flesh from the bone. The boiling should be done for a quarter of an hour at a time and the bones cleaned as much as possible after each boiling. In this way the relationship of the bones to one another can be noted and the small bones are less liable to be muddled up.

Some notes are given below to guide the student in the study of the skeleton. A general knowledge of the mammalian skeleton is assumed.

THE AXIAL SKELETON

(a) THE SKULL

The skull is composed of 41 bones.

The 'cartilage' bones form the sides and floor of the cranium, the posterior part of the palate, the hyoid and the ear ossicles. They are as follows :—

1 occipital (supraoccipital, basioccipital and exoccipitals fused together)
1 basisphenoid (basisphenoid and alisphenoids fused together)
1 presphenoid (presphenoid and orbitosphenoids fused together)
1 ethmoid forming the cribriform plate and part of the nasal septum
2 periotics surrounding the inner ear (mastoid and petrosal fused together)
2 palatines—part of the primitive mandibular arch
1 hyoid formed from the ventral part of the hyoid arch (basihyoid, ceratohyoids and thyrohyoids fused together ; the basihyoid—body ; ceratohyoids—anterior horns ; thyrohyoids—posterior horns)
2 malleus derived from the articular bones of the reptile and thus from the primitive mandibular arch
2 incus derived from the quadrate bones of the primitive mandibular arch
2 stapes derived from the hyomandibular bones of the hyoid arch.

The 'membrane' bones form the roof of the cranium and support the face. They are as follows :—

1 interparietal
2 parietals
2 frontals
2 nasals
2 lacrymals
4 turbinates
1 vomer
2 premaxillae
2 maxillae
2 jugals
2 squamosals
2 mandibles
2 tympanic bullae.

The dental formula of the rat is—I $\frac{1}{1}$; C $\frac{0}{0}$; PM $\frac{0}{0}$; M $\frac{3}{3}$ = 16.

THE FORAMINA OF THE SKULL

The skull has a number of foramina, the most important of which are listed below with notes on their position and the structures which pass through them.

*Group I—Foramina which perforate the wall of the cranium*

| FORAMEN | POSITION | STRUCTURES PASSING THROUGH IT |
|---|---|---|
| Foramen magnum | in occipital bone | spinal cord |
| Olfactory foramina | many in cribriform plate | olfactory nerves |
| Optic foramen | in orbitosphenoid region of presphenoid | optic nerve |
| Anterior lacerated foramen | between the bodies of the basisphenoid and presphenoid and the palatine | oculomotor, trochlear and abducens nerves and ophthalmic and maxillary branches of trigeminal nerve ; palatine branch of internal carotid artery out of cranium |
| Foramen ovale | in alisphenoid region of basisphenoid | mandibular branch of trigeminal nerve |
| Facial canal | in periotic | facial nerve |
| Internal auditory meatus | in periotic | auditory nerve |
| Posterior lacerated foramen | between periotic and occipital | glossopharyngeal, vagus and spinal accessory nerves ; internal jugular vein |
| Hypoglossal canal | in occipital | hypoglossal nerve |
| Post-glenoid foramen | between squamosal and periotic | vein from transverse sinus |
| Carotid canal | between basioccipital and periotic with a deep groove in the tympanic | main branch of internal carotid artery |
| Middle lacerated foramen | between alisphenoid region of basisphenoid and tympanic | pterygo-palatine branch of internal carotid artery out of cranium |
| Alisphenoid canal | in alisphenoid region of basisphenoid | palatine branch of internal carotid artery |
| Interpterygoid foramen | between palatine and basisphenoid | |

*Group II—Foramina which do not perforate the wall of the cranium*

| FORAMEN | POSITION | STRUCTURES PASSING THROUGH IT |
|---|---|---|
| Anterior palatine foramen | between premaxilla and maxilla in the palate | naso-palatine branch of trigeminal nerve |
| Posterior palatine foramen | in palatine | palatine branch of trigeminal nerve |
| Infra-orbital fissure | in maxilla in front of orbit | maxillary branch of trigeminal nerve and the anterior deep branch of the masseter muscle |
| Stylomastoid foramen | between periotic and tympanic | facial nerve from bulla |
| Posterior petro-tympanic foramen | between periotic and tympanic close to posterior lacerated foramen | pterygo-palatine branch of internal carotid artery into bulla |
| Petro-tympanic fissure | between periotic and tympanic | pterygo-palatine branch of internal carotid artery through bulla into cranium |
| Basisphenoid canal | in basisphenoid connecting with corresponding foramen of other side within the bone | pterygoid branch of internal carotid artery |
| Pterygo-palatine foramen | in basisphenoid from basisphenoid canal to wall of anterior lacerated foramen | pterygoid branch of internal carotid artery |
| Lacrymal groove | in lacrymal | naso-lacrymal duct |
| Eustachian canal | in tympanic | Eustachian tube |
| External auditory meatus | in tympanic | outer ear passage |
| Mandibular foramen | in inner side of lower jaw | mandibular branch of trigeminal nerve and mandibular blood-vessels |
| Mental foramen | in outer side of lower jaw | mental nerve |

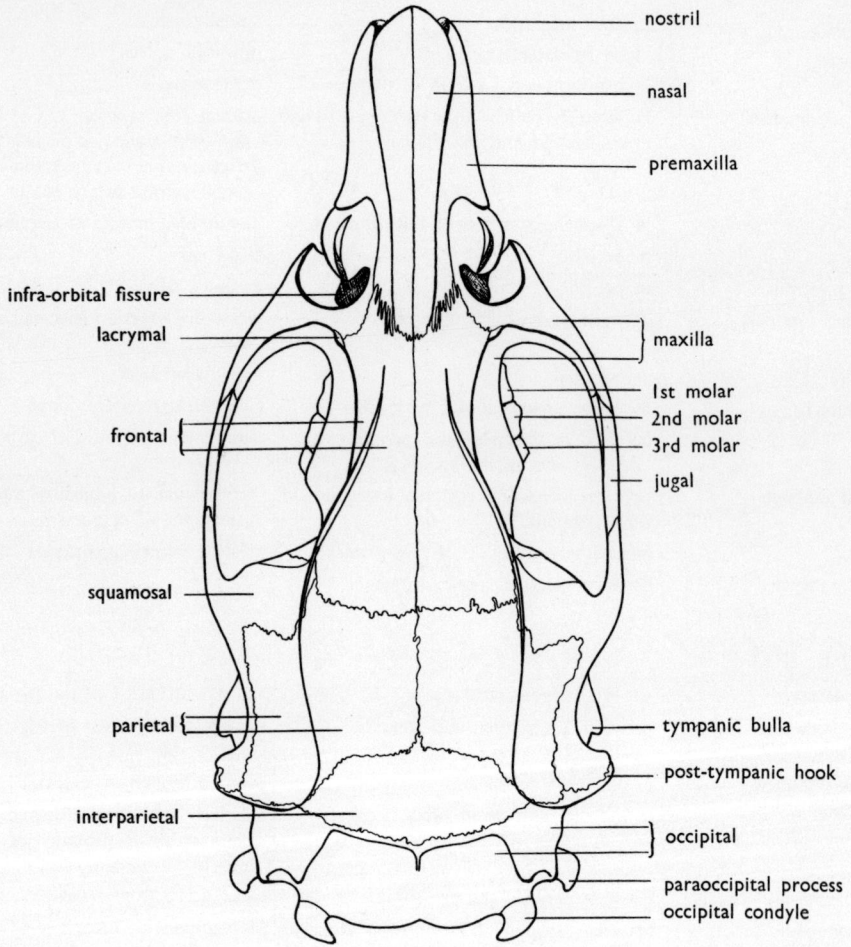

nostril

nasal

premaxilla

infra-orbital fissure

lacrymal

maxilla

1st molar

2nd molar

3rd molar

frontal

jugal

squamosal

parietal

tympanic bulla

post-tympanic hook

interparietal

occipital

paraoccipital process

occipital condyle

STANDARD × 5

SKULL (DORSAL ASPECT)

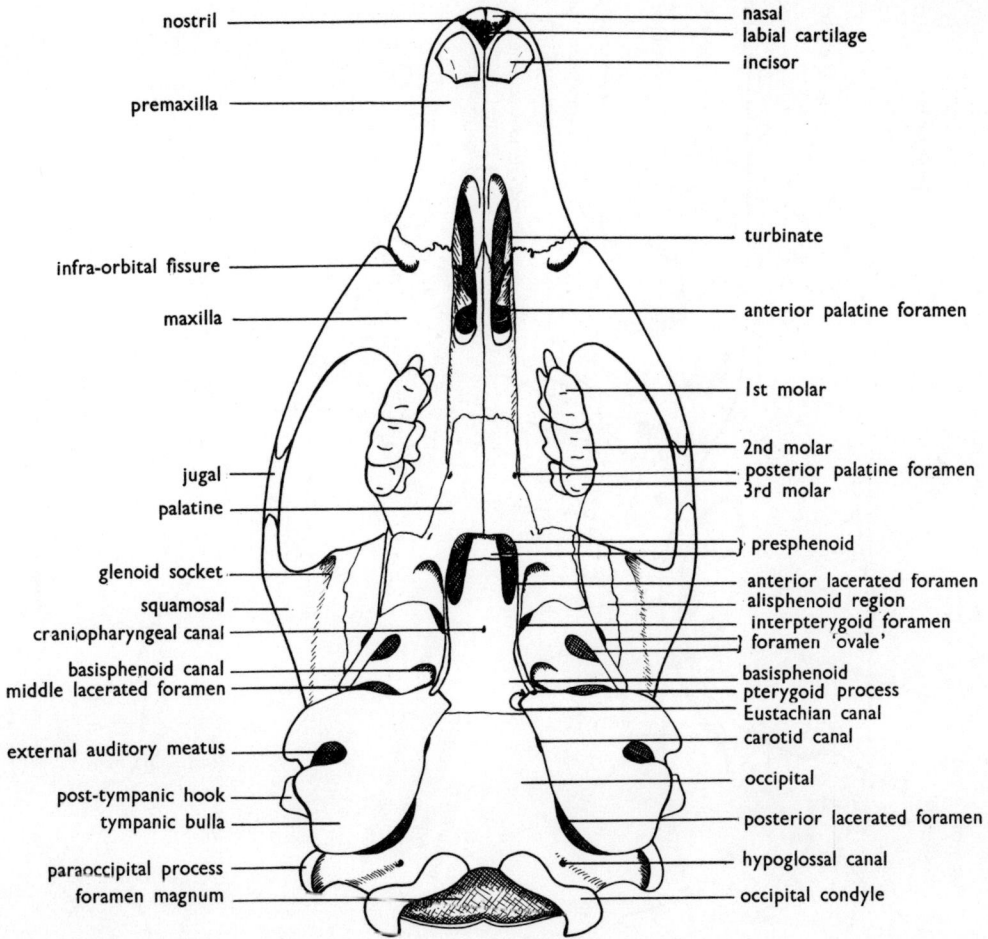

nostril — nasal
— labial cartilage
— incisor

premaxilla —

— turbinate

infra-orbital fissure —

maxilla — — anterior palatine foramen

— 1st molar

jugal — — 2nd molar
— posterior palatine foramen
palatine — — 3rd molar

— presphenoid
glenoid socket — — anterior lacerated foramen
squamosal — — alisphenoid region
craniopharyngeal canal — — interpterygoid foramen
— foramen 'ovale'
basisphenoid canal — — basisphenoid
middle lacerated foramen — — pterygoid process
— Eustachian canal
external auditory meatus — — carotid canal

post-tympanic hook — — occipital
tympanic bulla — — posterior lacerated foramen

paraoccipital process — — hypoglossal canal
foramen magnum — — occipital condyle

STANDARD × 5

SKULL (VENTRAL ASPECT)

49

*APPENDIX : THE SKELETON*

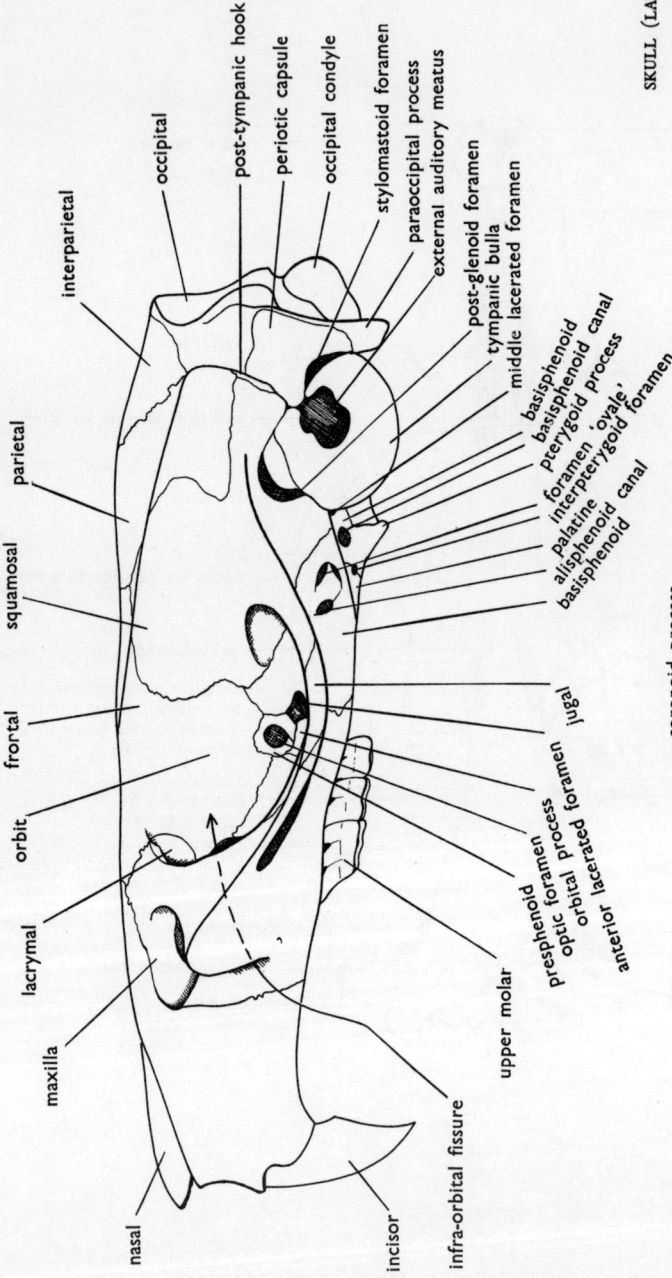

SKULL (LATERAL ASPECT)

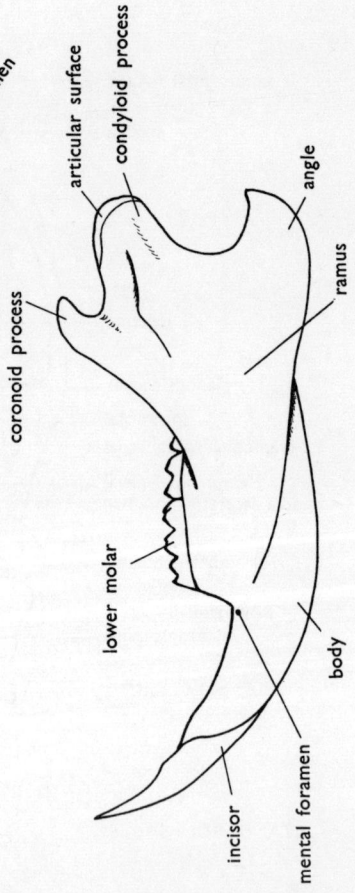

LOWER JAW (LATERAL ASPECT)

STANDARD × 5

APPENDIX : THE SKELETON

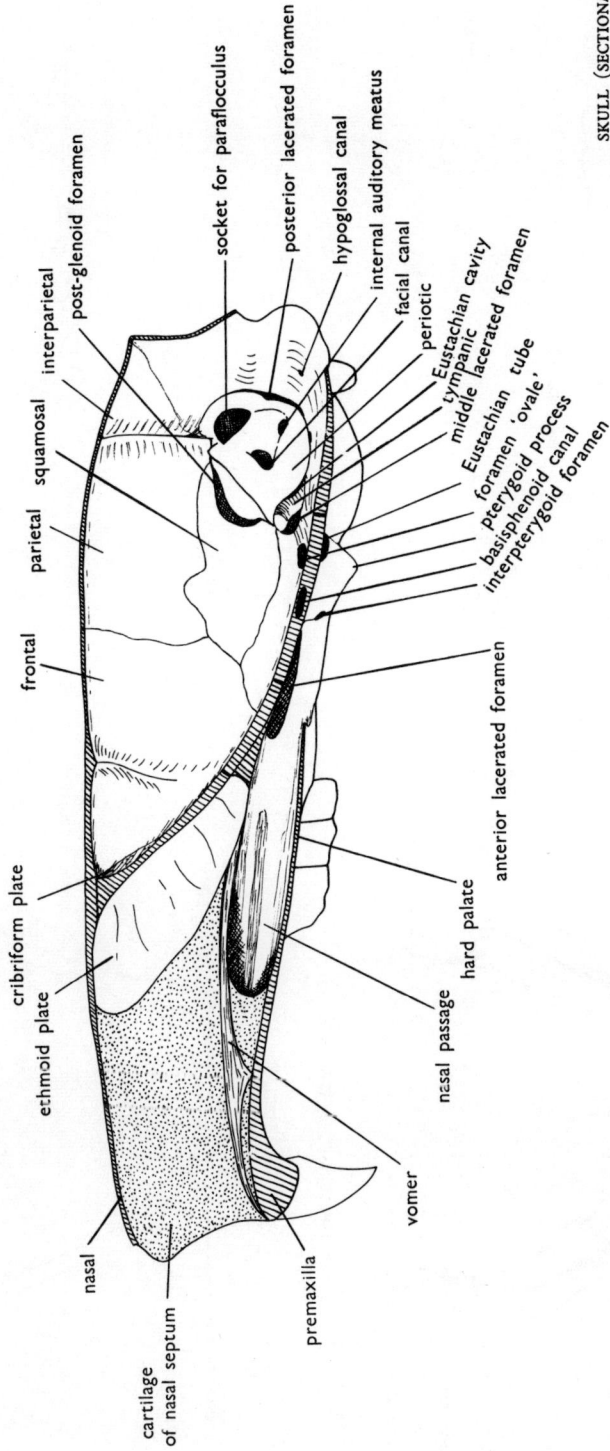

SKULL (SECTIONAL VIEW)

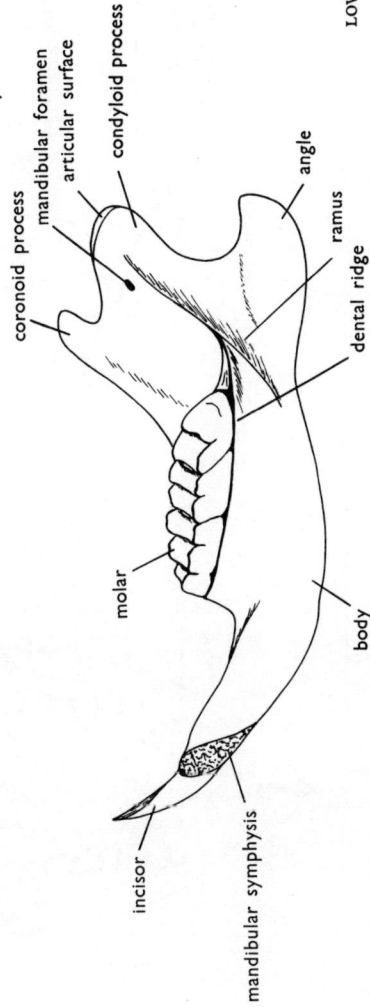

LOWER JAW (MEDIAL ASPECT OF ONE MANDIBLE)

STANDARD × 5

51

*APPENDIX : THE SKELETON*

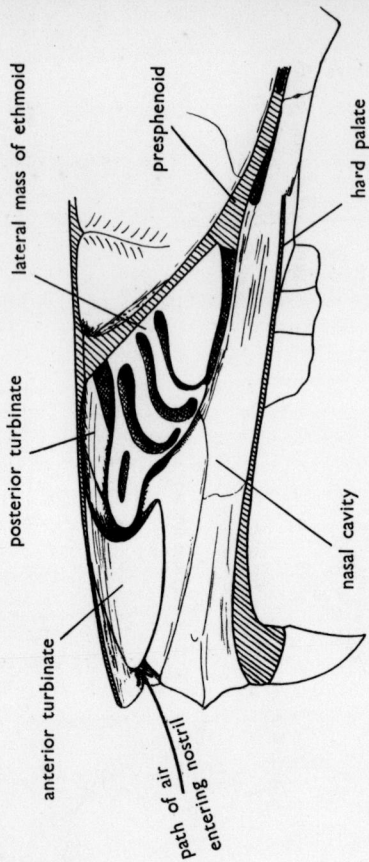

lateral mass of ethmoid

presphenoid

hard palate

posterior turbinate

nasal cavity

anterior turbinate

path of air entering nostril

NASAL CAVITY

STANDARD × 5

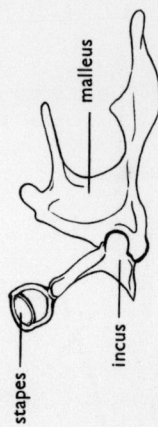

malleus

stapes

incus

AUDITORY OSSICLES

STANDARD × 25

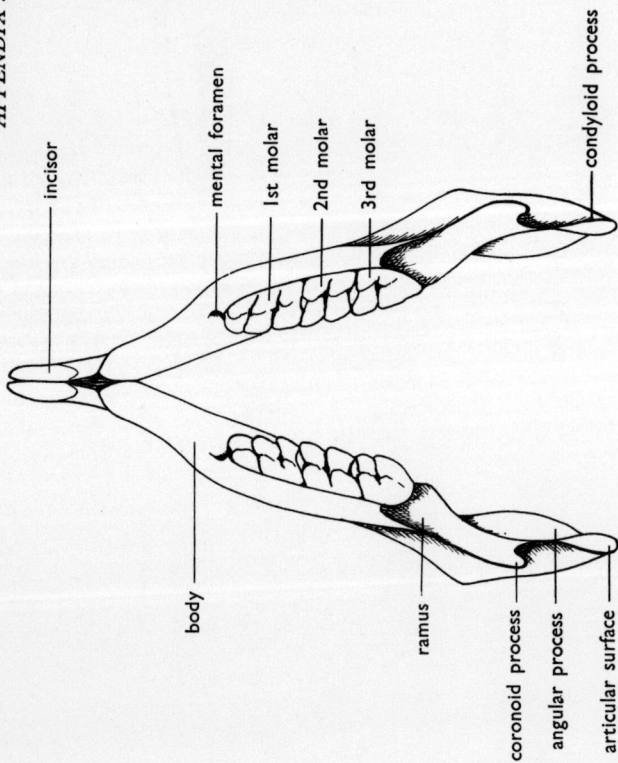

incisor

mental foramen

1st molar

2nd molar

3rd molar

condyloid process

body

ramus

coronoid process

angular process

articular surface

LOWER JAW (DORSAL ASPECT)

STANDARD × 5

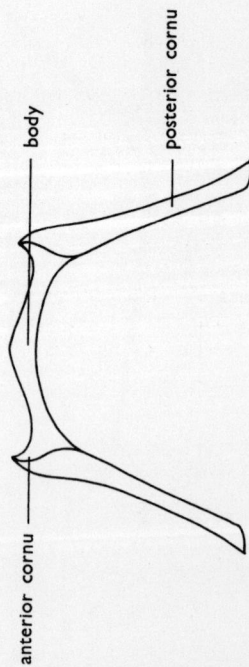

body

posterior cornu

anterior cornu

HYOID BONE

STANDARD × 10

(b) THE VERTEBRAL COLUMN

The rat has fifty-seven to sixty vertebrae which may be divided into five groups : cervical, thoracic, lumbar, sacral and caudal.

THE CERVICAL VERTEBRAE are characterized by the possession of vertebrarterial canals. These canals may be small or absent in the seventh cervical vertebra. Of the seven cervical vertebrae the first two are modified in the usual way as the atlas and axis. The ATLAS has articular surfaces for the occipital condyles of the skull and for the axis. It has no zygapophyses and no centrum. The AXIS has the odontoid peg, formed from the piece of bone which represents the missing centrum of the axis, often not fully fused on to its own centrum and thus clearly showing its origin. The axis has no prezygapophyses but postzygapophyses are present and the neural spine is long. The other five cervical are described as typical, but the sixth differs from the rest in the possession of enlarged cervical ribs.

THE THORACIC VERTEBRAE are characterized by their long neural spines and the articular facets for the heads and tubercles of the free ribs. There are thirteen thoracic vertebrae corresponding with the number of pairs of ribs. Of these vertebrae the second has a very long neural spine which articulates with a small triangular piece of bone, which is either the epiphysis of the neural spine or a sesamoid bone.

THE LUMBAR VERTEBRAE are characterized by the possession of anapophyses in addition to well-developed zygapophyses, transverse processes and neural spines. The transverse processes become progressively larger in the more posterior lumbar vertebrae. There are six of these vertebrae and with the exception of the sacral vertebrae they are the largest in the vertebral column.

THE SACRUM is formed of TWO SACRAL and TWO CAUDAL VERTEBRAE fused together. The transverse processes of the sacral vertebrae articulate with the ilia of the pelvic girdle. The vertebrae forming the sacrum are easily identifiable by their neural spines, the fused articular processes and the intervertebral canals between them. Complete fusion occurs only in old animals. In young rats the third and fourth vertebrae of the sacrum are free and resemble caudal vertebrae except for the absence of chevron bones.

THE FREE CAUDAL VERTEBRAE vary in number from twenty-seven to thirty. They vary in form progressively. The proximal ones show all the features of a typical vertebra and, but for the absence of anapophyses, closely resemble lumbar vertebrae. The gradual loss of all parts except the centrum is shown in the following table :—

| | |
|---|---|
| Complete vertebrae . . . . . . . . . . . . | 1 and 2 |
| Complete except for neural spines . . . . . . . . . . | 3 and 4 |
| With functional prezygapophyses but non-functional postzygapophyses and without neural spine | 5 |
| With non-functional pre- and postzygapophyses, without neural spines, but with distinct transverse processes . . . . . . . . . . . . . | 6–8 |
| With zygapophyses and transverse processes reduced to small knobs and without neural spines | 8–20 |
| With centra only . . . . . . . . . . . | 21–27 or 30 |

NOTE. Chevron bones are present in the tail, associated with the caudal vertebrae, but these are so small that they are usually lost when cleaning the skeleton.

THE INTERVERTEBRAL DISCS are very well developed. In the neck region they have two vertical ridges on each surface which fit vertical grooves on the centra of the vertebrae and in the tail region they have six radially arranged depressions into which fit knobs on the centra. These ridges, knobs and grooves prevent lateral slip of the bodies of the vertebrae. The centra of the thoracic vertebrae are almost flat, but here lateral movement is prevented by the heads of the ribs. In the lumbar region the intervertebral discs are firmly fixed to the anterior surfaces of the centra and are strongly convex where they fit into the concavity of the posterior surface of the adjacent vertebrae.

notch for 1st spinal nerve

transverse process

vertebrarterial canal

facet for axis

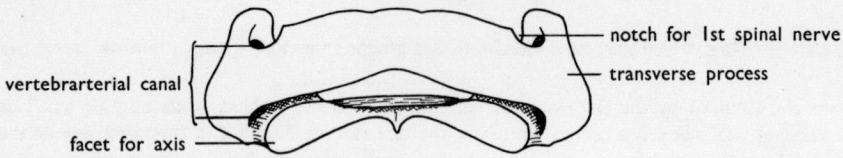

ATLAS (DORSAL ASPECT)

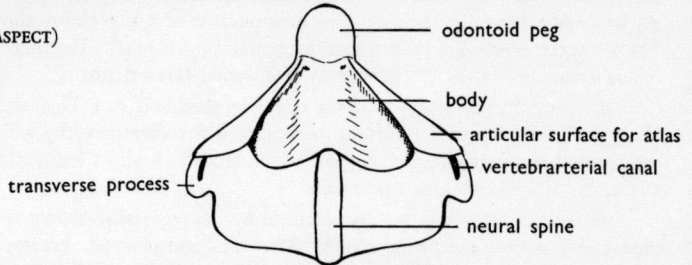

odontoid peg

body

articular surface for atlas

vertebrarterial canal

neural spine

transverse process

AXIS (DORSAL ASPECT)

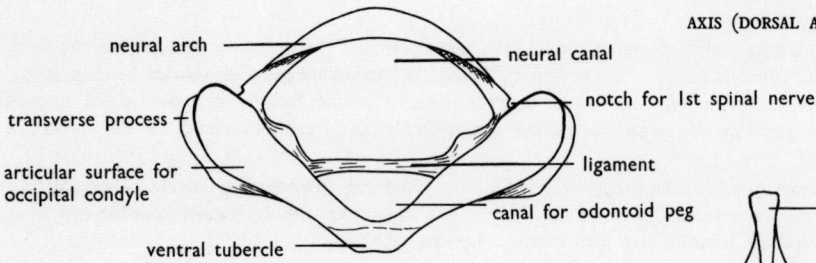

neural arch

neural canal

transverse process

notch for 1st spinal nerve

articular surface for
occipital condyle

ligament

canal for odontoid peg

ventral tubercle

ATLAS (ANTERIOR ASPECT)

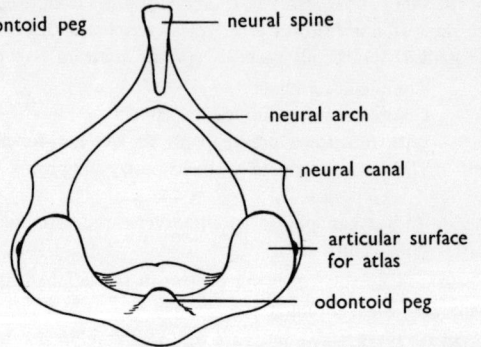

neural spine

neural arch

neural canal

articular surface
for atlas

odontoid peg

AXIS (ANTERIOR ASPECT)

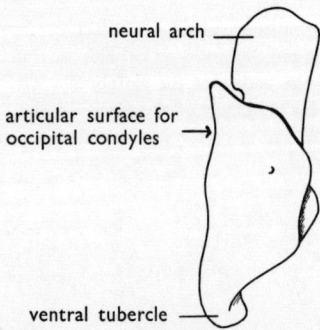

neural arch

articular surface for
occipital condyles

ventral tubercle

ATLAS (LATERAL ASPECT)

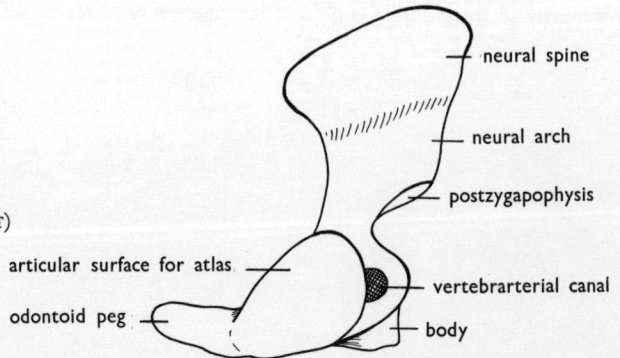

neural spine

neural arch

postzygapophysis

articular surface for atlas

vertebrarterial canal

odontoid peg

body

AXIS (LATERAL ASPECT)

STANDARD × 10

54

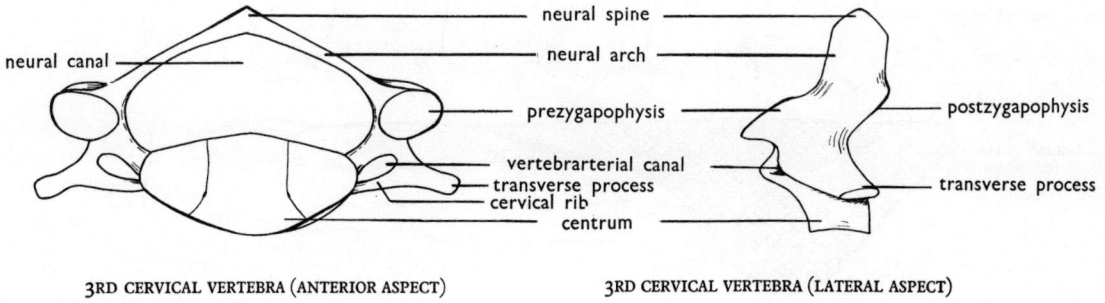

neural spine
neural arch
neural canal
prezygapophysis
postzygapophysis
vertebrarterial canal
transverse process
cervical rib
transverse process
centrum

3RD CERVICAL VERTEBRA (ANTERIOR ASPECT)     3RD CERVICAL VERTEBRA (LATERAL ASPECT)

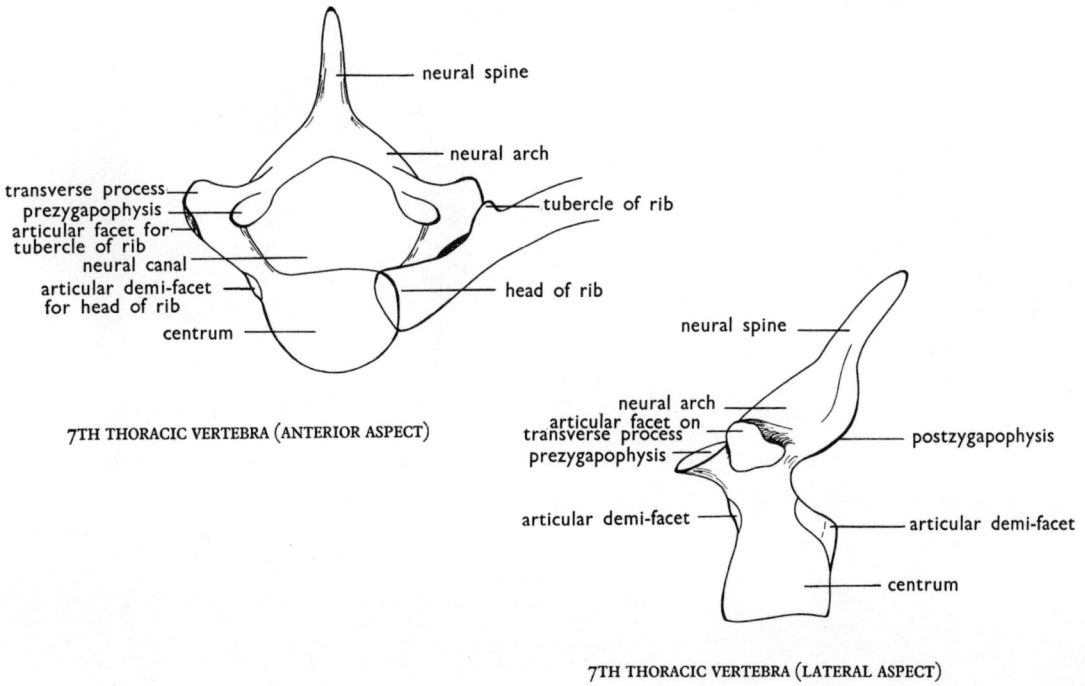

neural spine
neural arch
transverse process
prezygapophysis
articular facet for tubercle of rib
neural canal
articular demi-facet for head of rib
centrum
tubercle of rib
head of rib

7TH THORACIC VERTEBRA (ANTERIOR ASPECT)

neural spine
neural arch
articular facet on transverse process
prezygapophysis
postzygapophysis
articular demi-facet
articular demi-facet
centrum

7TH THORACIC VERTEBRA (LATERAL ASPECT)

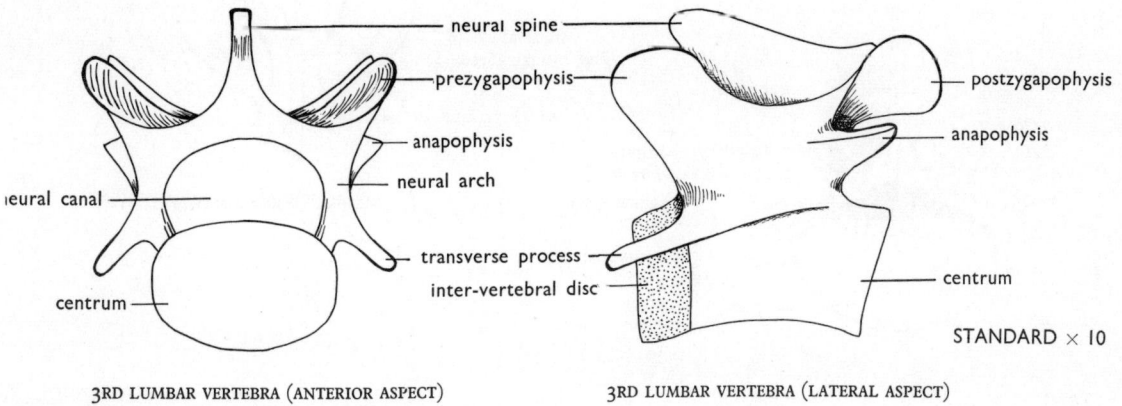

neural spine
prezygapophysis
anapophysis
neural arch
neural canal
transverse process
inter-vertebral disc
centrum
postzygapophysis
anapophysis
centrum

STANDARD × 10

3RD LUMBAR VERTEBRA (ANTERIOR ASPECT)     3RD LUMBAR VERTEBRA (LATERAL ASPECT)

neural spine

prezygapophysis

articular surface
for ilium

postzygapophysis

centrum

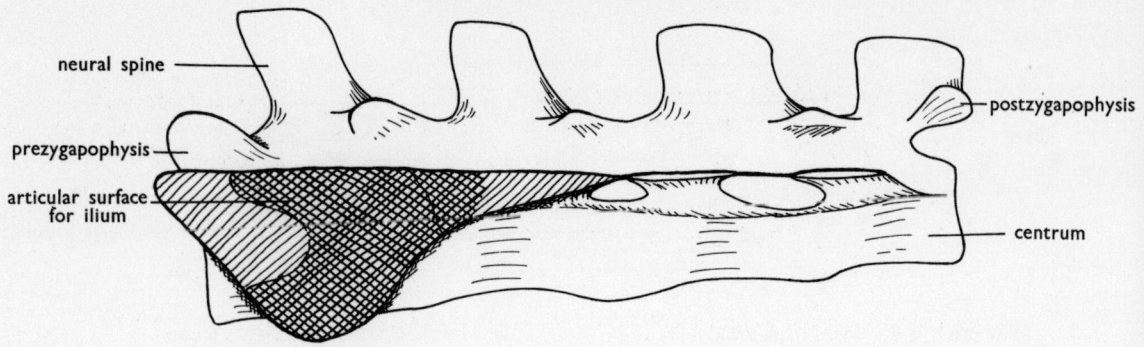

SACRUM (LATERAL ASPECT)

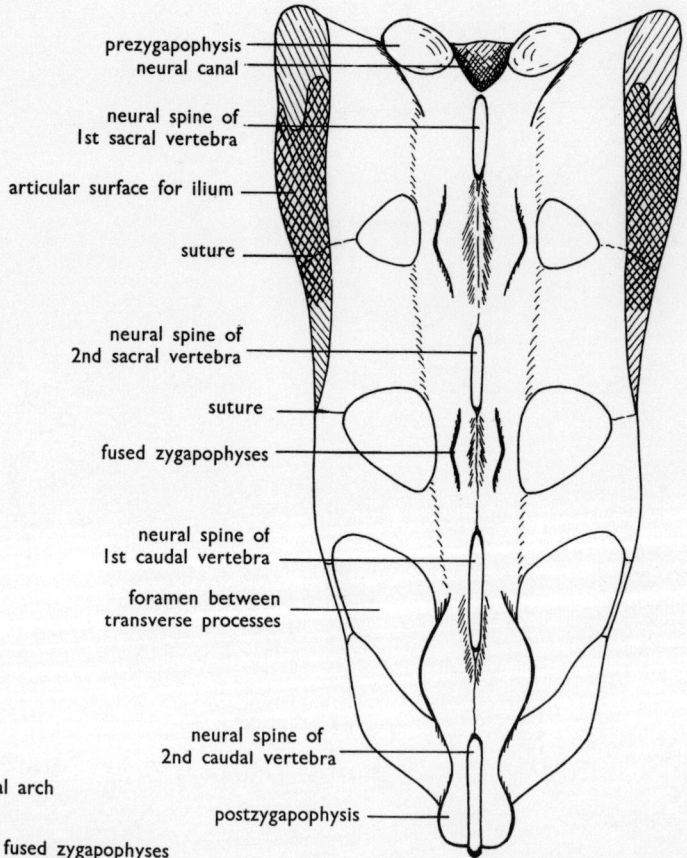

prezygapophysis
neural canal

neural spine of
1st sacral vertebra

articular surface for ilium

suture

neural spine of
2nd sacral vertebra

suture

fused zygapophyses

neural spine of
1st caudal vertebra

foramen between
transverse processes

neural spine of
2nd caudal vertebra

postzygapophysis

SACRUM (DORSAL ASPECT)

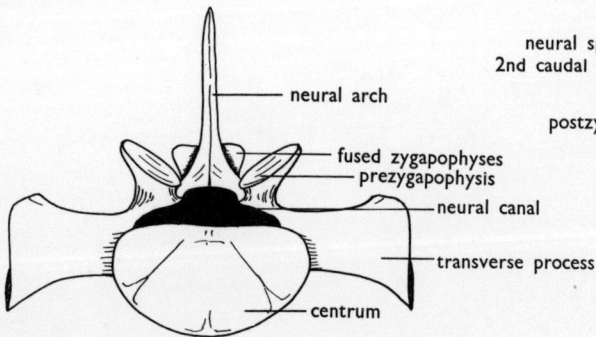

neural arch

fused zygapophyses
prezygapophysis

neural canal

transverse process

centrum

SACRUM (ANTERIOR ASPECT)

STANDARD × 10

56

prezygapophysis — postzygapophysis
neural canal — intervertebral notch
depression in — centrum
intervertebral disc
intervertebral disc
transverse process

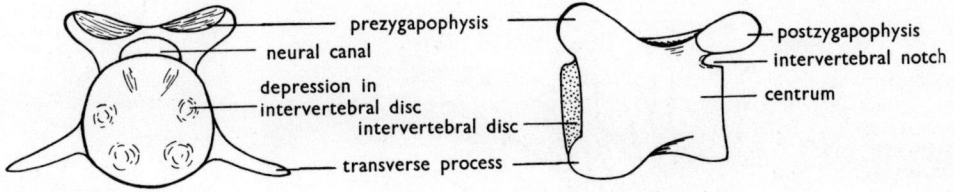

3RD FREE CAUDAL VERTEBRA (ANTERIOR ASPECT)    3RD FREE CAUDAL VERTEBRA (LATERAL ASPECT)

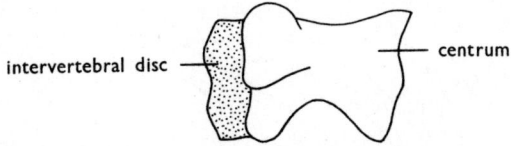

intervertebral disc — centrum

10TH FREE CAUDAL VERTEBRA (LATERAL ASPECT)

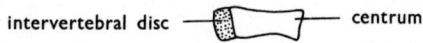

intervertebral disc — centrum

24TH FREE CAUDAL VERTEBRA (LATERAL ASPECT)

## APPENDIX : THE SKELETON

### (c) THE THORACIC CAGE

The thoracic cage is formed by the thirteen thoracic vertebrae, thirteen pairs of ribs and the sternum.

There are seven pairs of true ribs, and six pairs of false ribs of which three pairs are floating ribs.

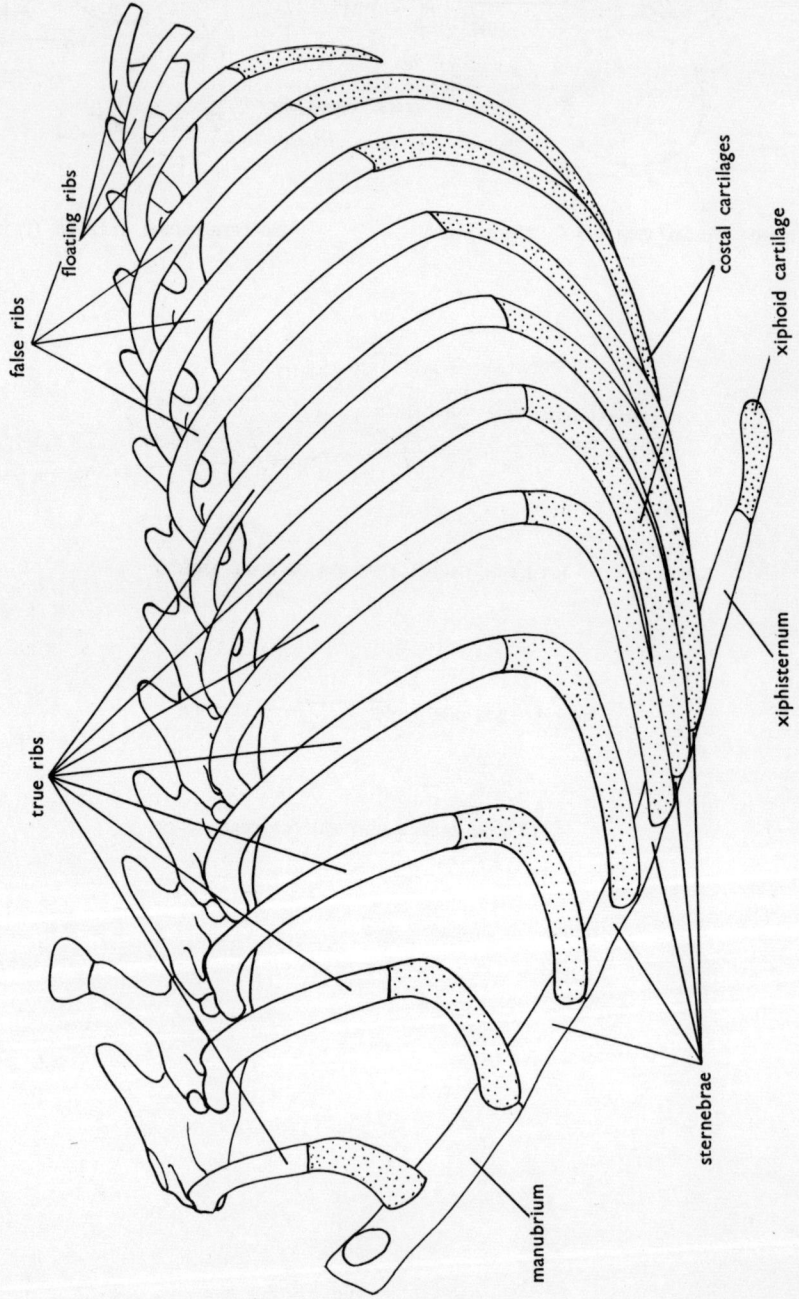

floating ribs

false ribs

costal cartilages

xiphoid cartilage

true ribs

xiphisternum

sternebrae

manubrium

THORACIC CAGE

STANDARD × 7

58

articular surface for pectoral girdle

articular surface for 1st costal cartilage

manubrium

sternebrae

xiphisternum

xiphoid cartilage

costal cartilages

tubercle

head

shaft

SECOND RIB

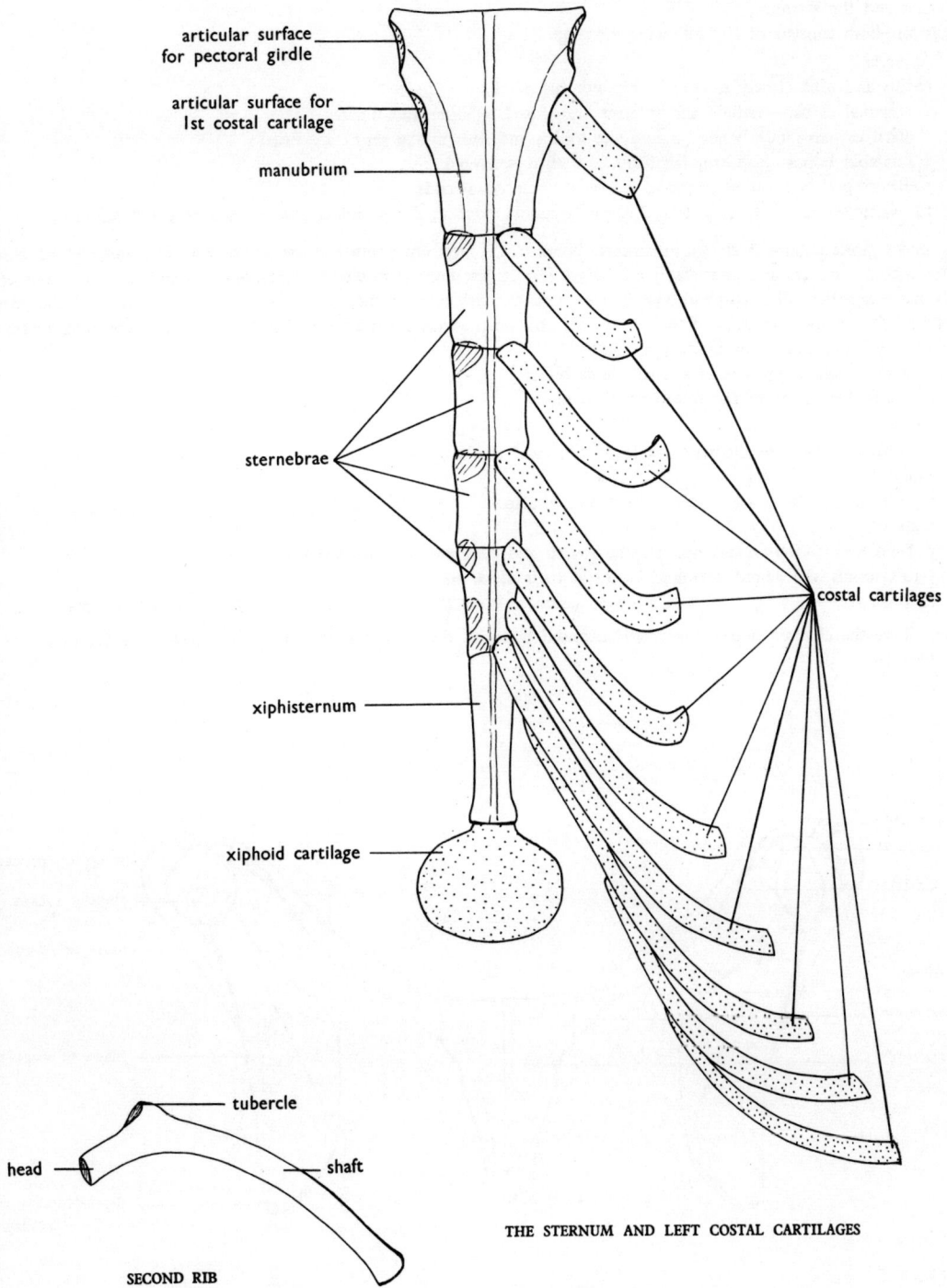

THE STERNUM AND LEFT COSTAL CARTILAGES

STANDARD × 7

### THE APPENDICULAR SKELETON

The pectoral girdle consists of two clavicles and two scapulae and vestiges of the procoracoids between them and between the clavicles and the sternum.

Each fore-limb consists of the following elements :

> humerus
> radius and ulna closely associated but not fused
> 2 proximal carpals—radiale and intermedium fused together and ulnare
> 5 distal carpals—four bones because the fourth and fifth in the series are fused
> 3 sesamoid bones—pisiform, falciform and ulnar sesamoid
> 5 metacarpals and paired sesamoid bones at their distal ends
> 14 phalanges—2, 3, 3, 3, 3, and a single sesamoid bone at the proximal end of each terminal phalanx

The pelvic girdle is formed of two innominate bones which meet one another at the pubic symphysis and each of which articulates with the sacrum at a sacroiliac joint. Each innominate bone is formed of four bones—ilium, ischium, pubis and cotyloid—fused together. The cotyloid bone is very small and lies between the other bones in such a manner that the pubis does not take part in the formation of the acetabulum, the deep socket for the head of the femur. The obturator foramen between each ischium and pubis is large.

Close to the pubic symphysis is a small penis bone.

Each hind-limb consists of the following elements :

> femur
> tibio-fibula formed of the partially fused tibia and fibula
> patella
> 3 proximal tarsals—tibiale, intermedium and fibulare
> centrale
> 5 distal tarsals—four bones because the fourth and fifth in the series are fused
> 5 metatarsals and paired sesamoid bones at their distal ends
> 14 phalanges—2, 3, 3, 3, 3, and a single sesamoid bone at the proximal end of each terminal phalanx

NOTE. Like the chevron bones, the small sesamoid bones of the hand and foot are generally lost during preparation of the skeleton.

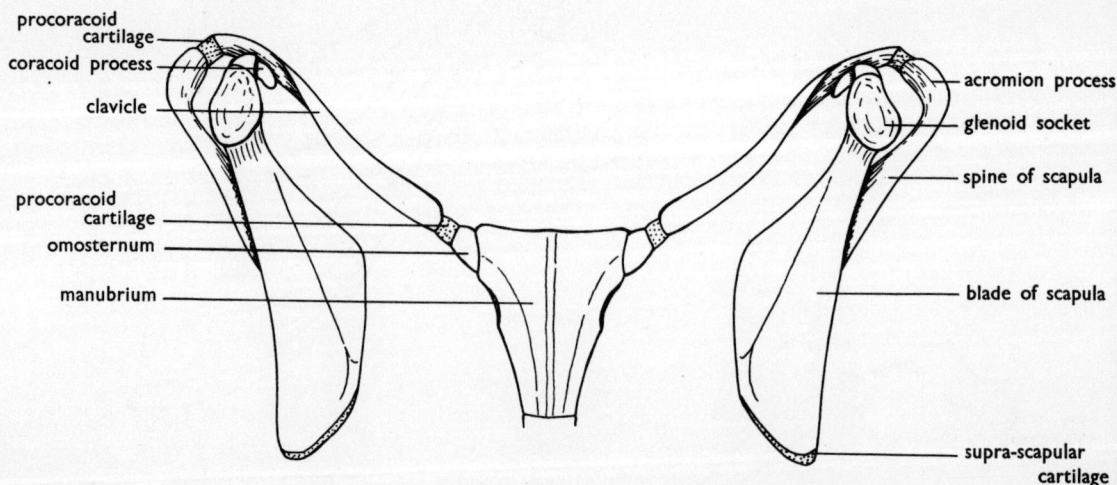

procoracoid cartilage
coracoid process
clavicle
procoracoid cartilage
omosternum
manubrium

acromion process
glenoid socket
spine of scapula
blade of scapula
supra-scapular cartilage

STANDARD × 5

PECTORAL GIRDLE (VENTRAL ASPECT)

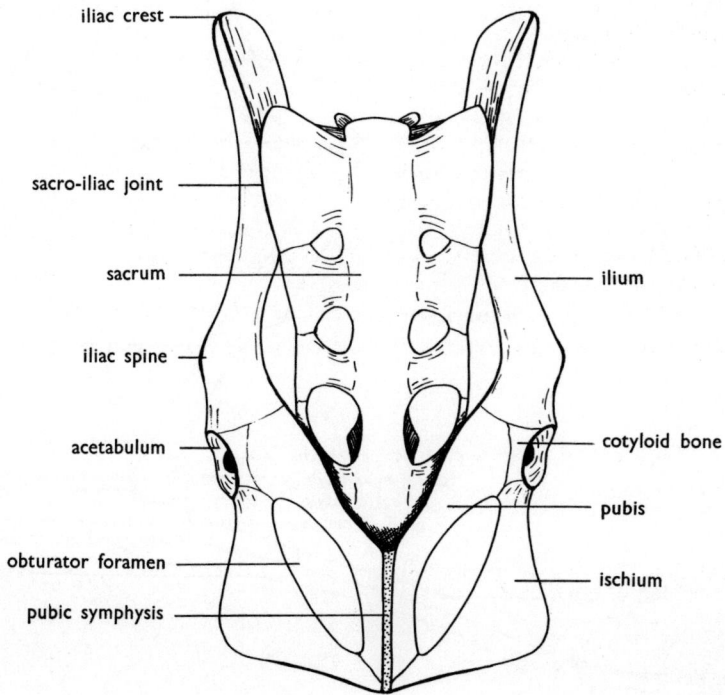

iliac crest

sacro-iliac joint

sacrum

iliac spine

acetabulum

obturator foramen

pubic symphysis

ilium

cotyloid bone

pubis

ischium

STANDARD × 5

PELVIC GIRDLE (VENTRAL ASPECT)

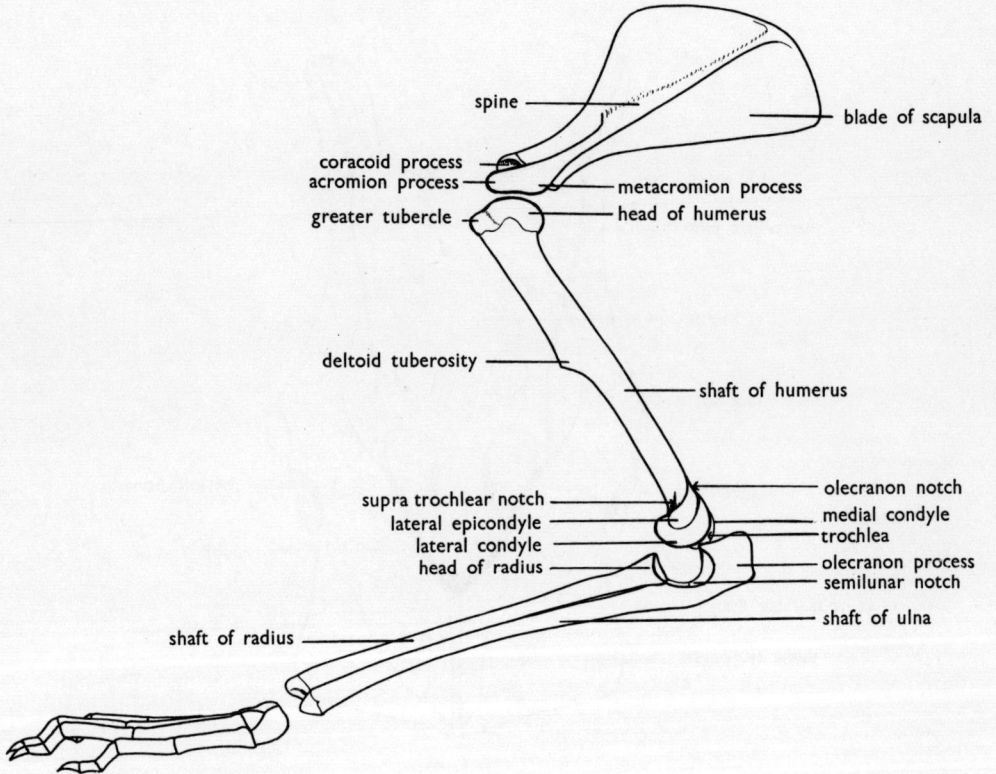

spine

blade of scapula

coracoid process
acromion process

metacromion process

greater tubercle

head of humerus

deltoid tuberosity

shaft of humerus

supra trochlear notch
lateral epicondyle
lateral condyle
head of radius

olecranon notch
medial condyle
trochlea
olecranon process
semilunar notch

shaft of radius

shaft of ulna

STANDARD × 5

LEFT FORE-LIMB AND SCAPULA, PARTIALLY DISARTICULATED (LATERAL VIEW)

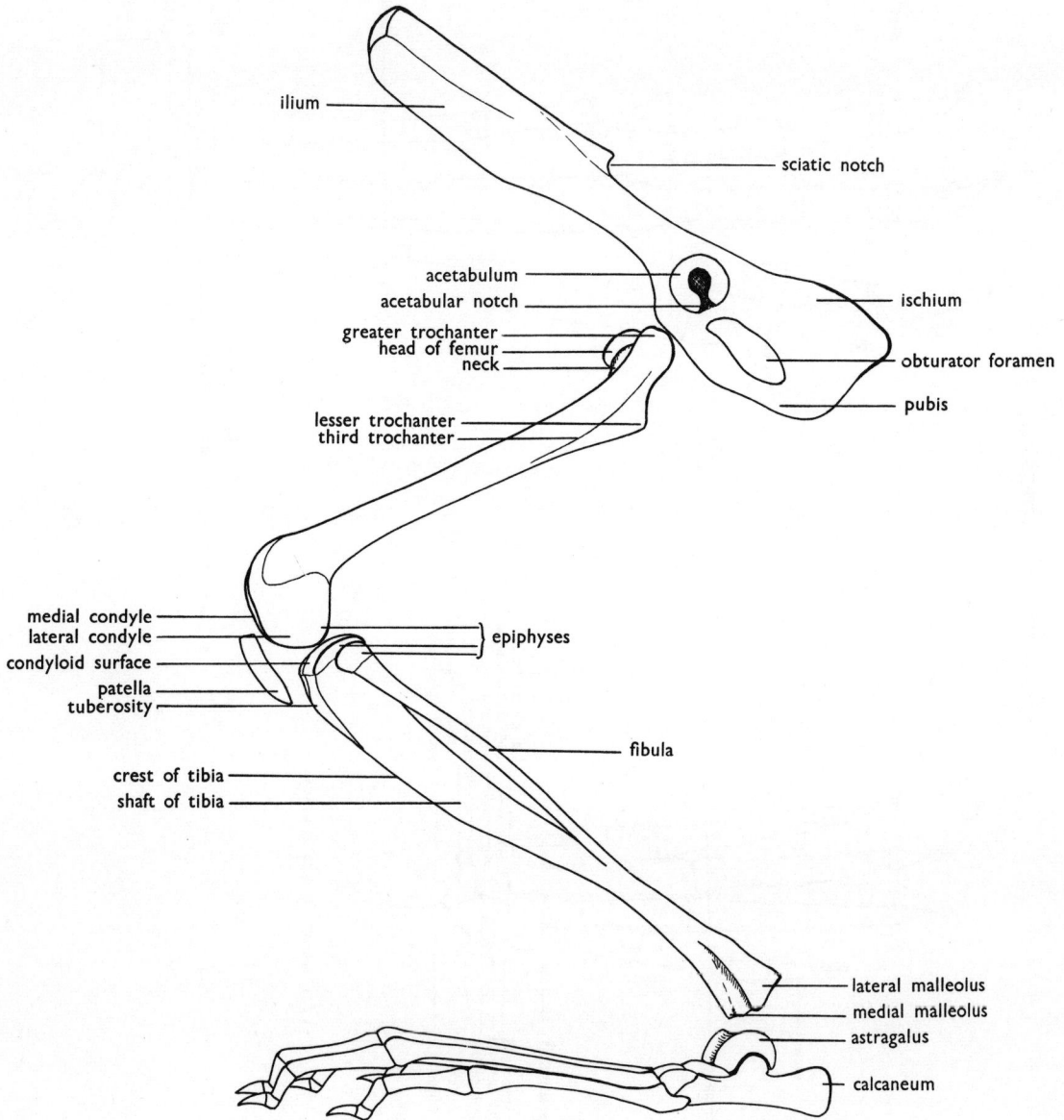

ilium

sciatic notch

acetabulum

acetabular notch

ischium

greater trochanter
head of femur
neck

obturator foramen

lesser trochanter
third trochanter

pubis

medial condyle
lateral condyle
condyloid surface
patella
tuberosity

epiphyses

fibula

crest of tibia
shaft of tibia

lateral malleolus
medial malleolus
astragalus
calcaneum

STANDARD × 5

LEFT HIND-LIMB AND PELVIS, PARTIALLY DISARTICULATED (LATERAL VIEW)

APPENDIX : THE SKELETON

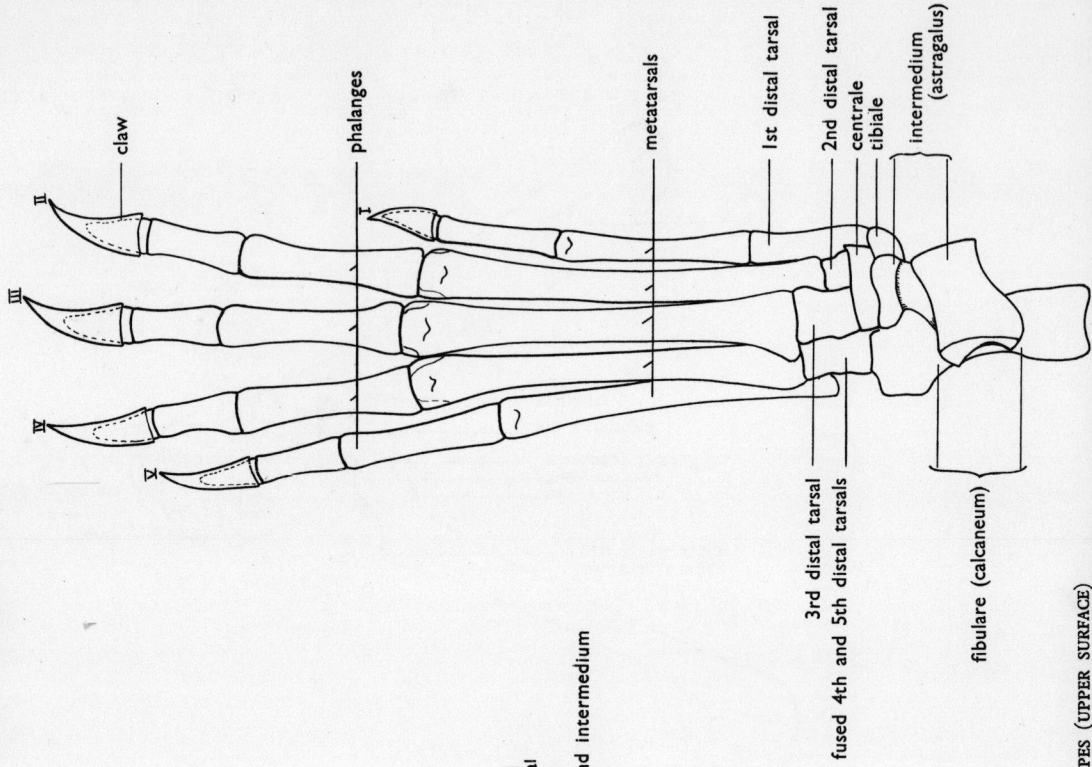

claw

phalanges

metacarpals

fused 4th and 5th distal carpals
ulnar sesamoid
3rd distal carpal
ulnare
ulnar epiphysis

1st distal carpal
2nd distal carpal
pisiform
centrale
fused radiale and intermedium
radial epiphysis

LEFT MANUS (UPPER SURFACE)

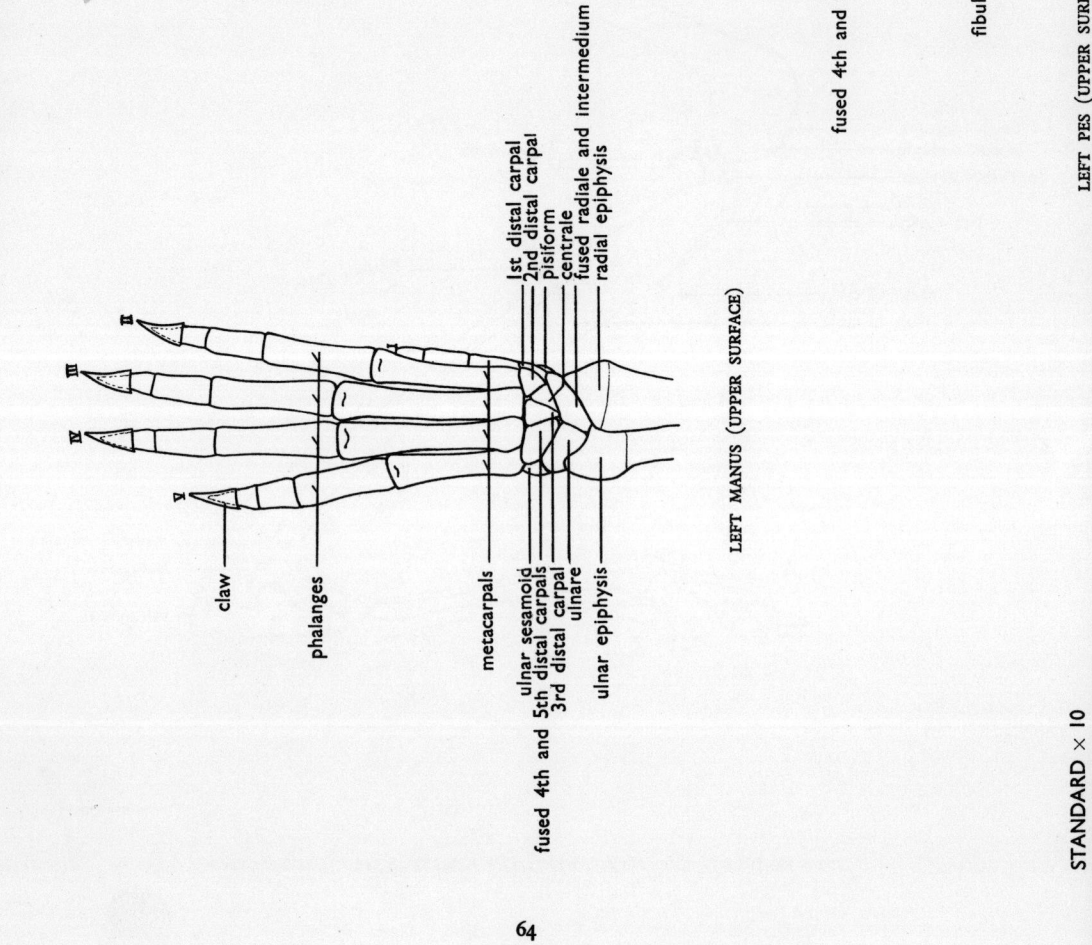

claw

phalanges

metatarsals

1st distal tarsal

2nd distal tarsal
centrale
tibiale
intermedium
(astragalus)

3rd distal tarsal
fused 4th and 5th distal tarsals

fibulare (calcaneum)

LEFT PES (UPPER SURFACE)

STANDARD × 10

64